Contents

Acknowledgements   6

Preface   7

Introduction   9

Chapter One
Leaps, Bounders and Kilts   17
Loch Spey to Laggan

Chapter Two
Hooks and Hooligans   27
Laggan to Newtonmore

Chapter Three
Shinty and Scallywags   35
Newtonmore to Kincraig

Chapter Four
Ospreys and a Plethora of Bridges   51
Kincaig to Nethybridge

Chapter Five
Battles and Boulders   63
Nethybridge to Ballindalloch

Chapter Six
Shortbread and Drams   73
Ballindalloch to Craigellachie

Chapter Seven
Soup, Salmon and Fiddles   85
Craigellachie to Fochabers

Chapter Eight
Ships, Picts and the Sea   97
Fochabers to Spey Bay

Appendices
One   Golf on Speyside   111
Two   Fishing on a budget   113
Three   The Story of Shinty   115
Four   Speyside for Whisky   117
Five   Flora and fauna of Speyside   119
Six   Useful websites   123

Acknowledgements

Thanks are due to a number of people for their help. Two books have been particularly useful as sources of information: *Discovering Speyside* by Francis Thomson (John Donald Publishers) and *Speybuilt* by Jim Skelton. Individuals who have assisted in a variety of ways include Aly Barr, Alex Black, Morag Hunter Carsch, Jane and Innes MacPherson, Peter Millar and Pat Till. We hope they know how much we appreciate it.

Most of the photographs were taken by the authors but it will be blindingly obvious that some are in a higher league altogether. David Whittaker at Spean Bridge took the wildlife photographs and Mark Williamson caught Strathisla Distillery on a beautiful snowy morning. Iain Carr contributed the front cover of the Spey at Orton and Bruce Macpherson the atmospheric image of Ruthven Barracks. Strathspey Railway allowed us to use their photograph of Glenbogle (aka Broomhill) station and Sight Savers International the image of Carron Bridge chosen by Annie Lennox. The Clan Macpherson Association allowed us to use the prize-winning photograph of the clan gathering. Fochabers Heritage gave permission to use photographs from their collection. Graeme Nairn allowed us to use his superb illustration from Jim Skelton's book, the original of which is owned by the Grants of Rothiemurchus.

Preface

This book started life as an illustrated talk which I have given to a large number of groups, schools and organisations in and around Moray. I broached the idea of a book with my brother Brian, but since I had never written down the text of the talk, Brian suggested he film me giving the talk to the Edinkillie WRI. This had the twin advantages of providing us with a text and with the kind of splendid supper enjoyed by guests of WRIs everywhere.

But obviously the text of a talk isn't a book. Jokes that work to a live audience tend to look foolish on the printed page; I occasionally allow the facts to defer to a good story and that's not allowed in print either; and a 90-minute talk would be a very slim volume indeed. Brian took on the job of greatly expanding this text, eliminating inaccuracies (unless you know differently!) and replacing some of the 'live' jokes with others that (we hope) work in print. That's why, although the book is written in the first person, we appear as joint authors.

We have also replaced my ageing slides with up-to-date photographs thanks to the wonder of the digital camera. I admit to being something of a technophobe, but the idea that you could take photographs on a sunny afternoon and be admiring them on a computer screen in the evening bowled me over. Maybe there's something to be said for this new-fangled technology after all!

I know it's been said before, but we've enjoyed writing the book, and we very much hope you enjoy reading it.

Donald Barr

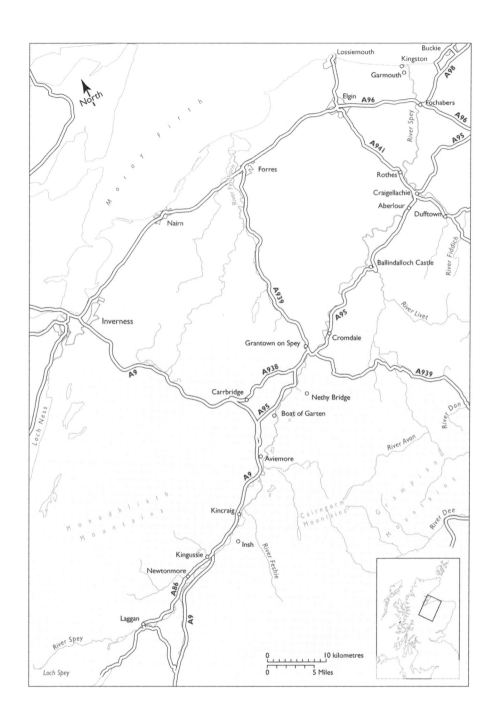

8   THE SPEY: FROM SOURCE TO SEA

Introduction

Can you love a river? I don't see why not. You can love a place, you can love a mountain, you can love a garden. So I am content to admit that I love the River Spey.

The affair started when, as a family, we spent every long summer in Newtonmore. My mother's family originated in nearby Glen Banchor. They were cleared out to make way for sheep in 1840 and moved down to the new town on the moor (hence Newtonmore), so even as youngsters, we felt a particular connection with Badenoch.

Until we became teenagers, my brother Brian and I were given a privileged status by local kids. They acknowledged that we weren't exactly natives, since we lived in Paisley the rest of the year, but our family links meant we weren't classed with the other visitors either. We snared rabbits with the locals, we swam in the River Calder with them, we were even – occasionally – allowed to join the *ad hoc* shinty games on the grass in front of the primary school.

The authors in Newtonmore with (centre) cousin John Calder

Our teens brought a natural end to all that. We joined the other holiday-makers playing tennis, going to dances, and driving in convoys to Loch Morlich, Feshiebridge and Loch Laggan for picnics.

Hard to believe now, but once we even managed to hitch a lift on the Inverness-London night train. We persuaded a couple of parents to drive a group of us to a weekend dance in Kingussie. On this lashing wet night after the dance we spoke to the station master at Kingussie who agreed to speak to the guard on the night train which was scheduled to stop there but not three miles later at Newtonmore. The driver agreed to slow down to a gentle walking pace at Newtonmore station so that we could safely step off. Perhaps it would be best not to try this today!

Perhaps you can remember how it was when these idyllic childhood holidays were coming to an end? After six weeks of fun and freedom and intense friendships, the prospect of going home to the city and back to the grim realities of school and tenements, the looming onset of autumn and winter, made the heart sink. One year, as the fateful morning dawned and our parents were packing the trunk and the suitcases, a knock came to the door. Calum Cattanach, a distant relative of our mother (and,

Father fishing the River Calder

Fishing where the Avon
meets the Spey at
Ballindalloch

incidentally, the only person with whom we ever heard our mother speak her
native Gaelic) had got up even earlier and fished a pool where the Calder meets
the Spey and was on the doorstep with two fine trout for us to take back south.
The fish not only held the promise of a splendid supper, their arrival provided
a perfect distraction from the heartbreak of the occasion.

These are my own early memories of the river. But I think the River Spey
means something to most Scots, and to many people from elsewhere. For some
it is the great salmon river, summoning up images of chaps in tweeds and
waders casting prodigious distances. To others the Spey is synonymous with
whisky. And others yet think of it as a fearsomely fast and dangerous river.

My parents were of this last school of thought. Strangely, they allowed us
to fish and swim unsupervised in the turbulent River Calder, but absolutely
prohibited doing the same in the Spey. They warned us of the dangers, of the
eddies and sudden drops in the bed of the river and, above all, of its sheer
speed. Fastest river in Scotland – they kept telling us – maybe the fastest in

Turbulent River Calder
emerging from
Glen Banchor

Britain, maybe even in the
whole of Europe. But this was a
puzzle for us because all we
could see was this big benign
river with ripples and wide
shallow pools and no danger
that we could fathom.

So is it so? Is the Spey the
fastest river in Scotland/Britain/
Europe? For the moment I can
only tell of a hitherto secret (sort
of) scientific (sort of) experiment

I conducted some years ago. I drove to Orton, between Rothes and Fochabers, where a track runs alongside the river. Leaving my engine running, I chucked a lump of wood into the middle, jumped in the car and drove alongside it. I had to do 12 or 13mph to keep up with the wood. It may not sound very impressive but a comparison with Europe's most fearsome river puts the Spey in perspective.

Orton, a site of special unscientific interest

Leisure sailors thinking of using the River Rhône as a route through France to the Mediterranean and back are solemnly warned of the dangers to navigation posed by the river's awesome speed, sometimes exceeding 6mph! It's a daunting thought, sure enough, in a small yacht that might manage 7mph flat out and sailors are warned not on any account to attempt to navigate up the Rhône unless their vessel can comfortably exceed this speed.

And there is another characteristic of the Spey which sets it apart from all the other major rivers in Scotland. Every important river has a city and/or a port at its mouth. The Ness has Inverness; the Dee and the Don have Aberdeen; the Tay has Perth and then Dundee; the Forth has Edinburgh and Leith; even the Tweed has Berwick, still a substantial town and port; and the Clyde has Glasgow and Greenock. And the Spey? Well, there's Inverspey. No? What about Aberspey, then? No? At its mouth the Spey has the villages of Garmouth, Kingston and Tugnet. Lovely little places in their own quiet way, but none would lay claim to being a town, far less a city or a port.

The reason is that the Spey declines to behave in the way that rivers are expected to behave as they approach the sea. Rivers slow down into great, sedate waterways as they near their end. The word 'majestic' should apply, and often the local university rowing club will use such rivers to practise their skills. Any students trying that on the Spey as it nears the sea would find themselves halfway across the Moray Firth before they finished the first verse of *Gaudeamus igitur*.

It isn't only the speed of the river that made it impossible to build a substantial town at its mouth. The Spey can't make up its mind which is the best route to the sea. Over its last mile or two, the main channel moves unpredictably from the west side at Kingston to the Spey Bay side. It's hard to build a town where there is no way of knowing for certain where the river ends and the land begins.

But, going back to the matter of speed, the Spey might have ended its journey in a respectably calm state but for the intervention of a river which really has no right to be where it is.

A series of photographs showing the Spey Viaduct with the river dithering about the best route to the sea. Bottom image is the most recent with the main river now on the Spey Bay side.

The River Avon (pronounced A'an, by the way) starts life at Loch Avon, nestled between Cairn Gorm and Ben Vain in the heart of the Cairngorms. It sets off confidently eastwards and comes within a mile or two of meeting the headwaters of the Don which would have taken it

12

down to join the North Sea at Aberdeen. But the glacier which set its path suddenly turned sharp left and headed North instead; so the Avon follows suit and meets the Spey at Ballindalloch, which is just about where the Spey should be thinking that the tumultuous part of its journey was over and it could settle into a dignified middle age. In actual fact, the Avon doesn't so much meet the

Spey as smash into it. The Spey has to try to absorb a sudden 50 per cent increase in volume. Left to its own devices the river would simply break its banks. But this section of the Spey has been heavily engineered to prevent flooding, so the only way it can shift all this water is by speeding up when by rights it should be slowing down.

And that is why neither Inverspey nor Aberspey has come into being.

Note this, too. Most major rivers have a substantial market town about halfway between source and sea. Inverurie on the Don; Perth on the Tay; Stirling on the Forth; take your pick of Galashiels, Melrose and Kelso on the Tweed; Lanark on the Clyde. There is the perfect spot for a substantial market town on the Spey: a lovely wide strath north east of Kingussie, excellent agricultural land which should be able to support dozens of farms providing the basis for a market town. The problem is another troublesome tributary, in this case the Feshie.

Most of the time the Feshie is just another modest Highland river

and the Spey has no trouble absorbing it, as it does the Truim, the Tromie, the Mashie, the Calder and all its other early tributaries. The problem with the Feshie is that its catchment area includes the Moine Mhor, the great mossy plateau towering 3,000–4,000ft above Glenfeshie at the southern end of the Cairngorms. Given a spring thaw, the combination of snow melt and rainfall turns the

Spey Bay, site of the city-that-never-was

The Feshie goes a wee bit mad

Feshie into a mad thing carrying so much water that even the mature Spey struggles to get past the torrent. In this case there's only one thing the Spey can do and that's back up, sometimes up to a height of five feet and all that prime agricultural land upstream is flooded. It turns into the Insh Marshes, a paradise for wading birds, and quite hopeless for farming. Mind you, if global warming does what many experts expect, the Insh Marshes might one day become a major source of rice!

Anyway, here is the River Spey from the small brown trout of Loch Spey to the dolphin pods of the Moray Firth, from a meagre little burn high in the Monadhliath Mountains to a powerful waterway nearly 100 miles later.

This is the Spey, from source to sea.

Top and Middle: **Insh Marshes – Scotland's rice bowl?**

Above: **The difference 100 miles makes...**

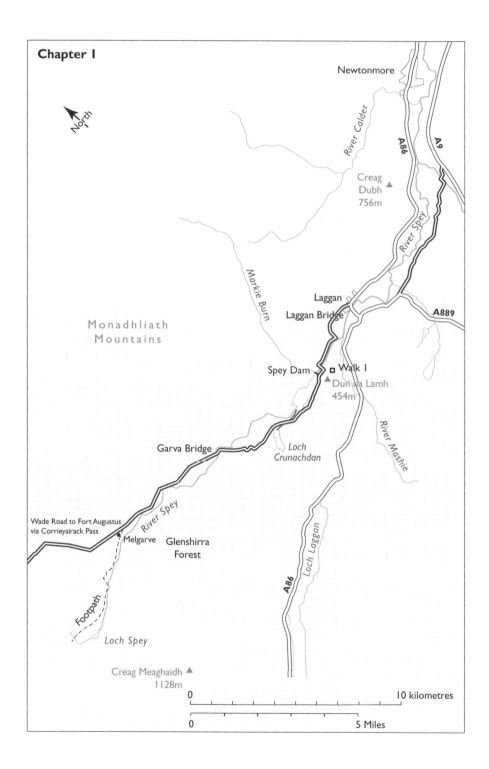

Newtonmore

North

River Calder

A86

A9

Creag
Dubh
756m

River Spey

Markie Burn

Monadhliath
Mountains

Laggan
Laggan Bridge

A889

Spey Dam

Walk 1

Dun na Lamh
454m

River Mashie

Garva Bridge

Loch
Crunachdan

Wade Road to Fort Augustus
via Corrieyairack Pass

River Spey

Melgarve

Glenshirra
Forest

A86

Loch Laggan

Footpath

Loch Spey

Creag Meaghaidh
1128m

0   10 kilometres

0   5 Miles

Chapter One

Leaps, Bounders and Kilts

Loch Spey to Laggan

In all my childhood holidays in Badenoch, I never got around to tracing the Spey back to its source, so when I moved to live in Moray I had my opportunity. Turn off the old A9 (now the A86) at Newtonmore on to the Laggan road. Turn right again at Laggan and on to General Wade's road to Garva Bridge. A few miles beyond the bridge, the Spey eases away to the south west and a rough path on the north bank leads to Loch Spey, a typical small Highland loch lying in the shadow of the 'wrong' side of Creag Meaghaidh (the 'right' side includes Coire Ardair, a Mecca for snow and ice climbers).

And there, at the east end of the loch, is the unprepossessing little burn that is the Spey. I make a small claim to fame. On an early visit, with the burn no more than a trickle, I stood astride the Spey and had a widdle in the middle. Surely a world first! But on a more recent visit the trickle had become much wider and deeper because of heavy rain. But I still wanted to be the first person – perhaps –

Top:
Loch Spey

Bottom:
**Hinds, not stags,
near Loch Spey**

to leap the Spey in one bound. I got about halfway across and arrived, wet and deflated, on the far bank. So I have to settle for being the first person – perhaps – to land halfway across the Spey and live to tell the tale! I not only failed in my leap, I also left the scene in some disarray.

The bleak and soggy moorland surrounding Loch Spey and the rough walk in from the Wade road means this is not a place that draws crowds of visitors. But it is not uninhabited.

The place is full of deer, and on this occasion I had turned up in the middle of the rutting season. The roaring and clashing of antlers was some way off as I set up my little tent and prepared to turn in for the night. An hour or two later I was

Cathal's Stone

wakened by the noise – much closer now – and I could feel the ground trembling under me as the warring stags fought all around. I poked my head out of the tent and I did not like what I saw. The stags were just yards away and they were so focused on their primeval combat they were oblivious to the presence of the flimsy tent and its nervous occupant. Bugger this, I thought, and I packed up my gear and set off back down the path to spend the night in my car. The stags had neither noticed my presence, nor my craven departure.

There is a standing stone (left) – or, more accurately, a sinking stone – on the moor between the fledgling Spey and Wade's road. It is marked as Clach na Cathalainn (Cathal's Stone) on OS maps but only about two feet of the stone remain above ground and there are two entirely contradictory stories about its origins.

It may mark the site of the battle of Garva, 1187, between competing claimants to the Scottish throne, Donald Ban and William the Lyon. Donald lost not only the battle, but his head.

Or, more romantically, it marks the burial place of a young Irishman, Cathal, who eloped with the daughter of Cluny MacPherson. The lovers spent the night in a nearby cave, but Cluny's retainers tracked them through the snow, murdered the young Irishman and brought back the daughter. When they discovered that Cathal was of high birth and would, in fact, have made a perfectly acceptable husband, the MacPhersons erected the stone over his grave.

General George Wade was appointed Commander-in-Chief, North Britain by George I in 1724 with the specific remit of reporting to the king on the best way of controlling and disarming the Highlands following the Jacobite uprisings of 1689, 1715 and 1719. He reported succinctly that almost all Highlanders capable of bearing arms were ready to use them against the Crown.

Wade bridge and road

His solution was to build a network of barracks, roads and bridges to allow the King's army to move quickly to quell any agitation.

Wade's roads linked Stirling, Perth, Inverness, Fort William and Fort Augustus and it was his road linking Speyside with Fort Augustus, over the 2,500ft high Corrieyairack Pass that had taken me close to Loch Spey. The road may not be quite

THE SPEY: FROM SOURCE TO SEA

up to motorway standard these days, but its foundations were well laid by the hundreds of conscripts who worked on it and it is still a great improvement on the rough muddy footpaths that preceded it. The double-span Garva Bridge, completed in 1733, is its most prominent – and most photographed – feature.

Wade himself celebrated the opening of the new road by driving over it in a coach drawn by six horses, much to the amazement of the locals who had never seen such a conveyance.

Further down the road, at Garvamore, are Wade's barracks. General Sir John Cope might prefer the building to disappear

into a deep hole, for it marks one of his less than heroic moments as an army commander.

In 1745, Cope was sent with a force of 4,000 well-armed soldiers, many of them mercenaries from mainland Europe, to meet the Jacobite forces under Bonnie Prince Charlie coming South following the raising of his standard at Glenfinnan. The Hanoverian troops gathered at the Garva barracks ready to meet the oncoming enemy. Cope sent his scouts ahead to report on the strength of the 'rebels'. When they came back they had, as they say, good news and bad news.

Top:
Garva Bridge
Middle:
Garvamore Barracks
Bottom:
Highland attack at Prestonpans
image from Britishbattles.com

The good news was that the Jacobites were lightly armed with nothing more than claymores, dirks and targes. The bad news was that they seemed very much at home in the inhospitable landscape, unlike Cope's shivering, miserable troops. Cope suddenly remembered an urgent appointment he and his men had in Inverness and left the rebel army to get on with their campaign

unmolested. When he finally met up with the Prince later in the year at Prestonpans, Cope might have done well suddenly to remember another appointment. Instead he not only led his troops to total rout, but by leading the retreat he also became the first general in history to bring news of his own defeat. But at least the event gave the Jacobites a fine stirring folk song with which to remember him.

> Hey, Johnnie Cope, are ye wauking yet?
> Or are your drums a-beating yet?
> If ye were wauking I wad wait
> To gang to the coals i' the morning

A little further down towards Laggan, the Spey reaches a dam – imaginatively called Spey Dam – where the river is divided in two. One half continues on its way towards the distant Moray Firth. The other half turns back on itself and makes an extraordinary journey to the British Aluminium – now called British Alcan – smelter at Fort William.

A canal links with nearby Loch Crunachdan, then a pipeline carries the Spey water to Loch Laggan then to Loch Treig and finally by a 15 mile pipeline to emerge from the side of Ben Nevis and down to the smelter. For some 50 years after it was completed in 1929, this was the longest water supply tunnel in the world. Once British Alcan has finished with it, this half of the Spey ends

Spey Dam and Dun na Lamh

THE SPEY: FROM SOURCE TO SEA

up in Loch Lochy and thence down Neptune's Staircase to the sea at Loch Linnhe. So here's a question for the pub quiz: Which river flows into both the Atlantic Ocean and the North Sea?

The fort and some of the 16,000 rocks ... and not a Rhinemaiden in sight

An equally impressive – if rather older – piece of civil engineering overlooks Spey Dam. If the steep conical hill above the dam were, instead, overlooking the Rhine, you'd expect a Disney-style castle on top and, perhaps, a Rhine maiden or two draped around the place singing the odd snatch of Wagner. But this is Scotland, so instead you have Dun na Lamh, a massive Pictish fort. It consists of 16,000 rocks – no, I don't know who counted them – and the rocks come in two sizes: grown man-size and boy/woman-size. It is truly humbling to imagine the effort that went into building the fort, which begs the question: who were they defending themselves against?

There is no doubt about the fort's strategic position. It overlooks Strathmashie and the route south to Perth, Strathspey and the route north to Inverness and the only route through to the west via the Corrieyairack. But the Romans never came this far inland and neither did the Vikings. The likely answer is that the Picts were defending themselves against the Scots, the Gaelic-speaking interlopers from Ireland who eventually colonised most of the west and north of Scotland.

It is worth noting that these earlier Celts, the Picts, spoke a Brythonic language that was closely related to Welsh and to Cornish, Breton and the old language of Galicia in north west Spain. Take just one example. The Gaelic for the mouth of a river is *Inver*, as in Inverness; in Welsh it is *Aber*, as in Aberystwyth. Or Aberdeen. Or, on the course of the Spey, Aberlour.

Finally comes the village of Laggan which promotes itself as *Monarch of the Glen* country after much of the BBC series was filmed in and around the

village. By now the Spey has been joined by several substantial burns and by the River Mashie, so Laggan Bridge is crossing a rather self-assured river.

Laggan church was built in 1785 and its first minister was the Rev. James Grant. But it was Grant's wife Anne who had the greater impact on the life of Scotland, the effects of which continue to the present day.

Anne Grant was a prolific letter-writer and her descriptions of the reality of Highland life upset all of the contemporary stereotypes. It was generally believed that Highlanders were pagan, uncouth, uneducated, dirty and savage. Anne Grant painted a quite different picture. She reported that they were, in fact, deeply religious, educated enough to read the Bible in Gaelic, hospitable, and

Top:
Laggan Church
Middle:
Anne Grant by Augustin Edouart
National Galleries of Scotland

rather noble. Her letters were published in 1808 as *Letters from the Mountains* and the book became a best-seller. Sir Walter Scott was greatly impressed by her account of Highland life and his rather romanticised version of the Highlands became a staple of his novels.

In a letter dated Laggan, 5 July 1786, Anne Grant describes roups, or sales, of a family's goods and cattle on the death of the head of the household where it was the custom for kinfolk from the surrounding counties to buy the livestock at inflated prices in order to help the grieving family. The sale is followed by a dinner.

> Whether it can be afforded or not, there is always a plentiful dinner
> and very plentiful drink on these occasions, which the friendly
> greetings of so many people, bound by a common tie, frank, lively,
> and not deficient in that good breeding which habitual kindness
> and courtesy forms, render no unpleasing scene to those who
> witness the conclusion of it.

THE SPEY: FROM SOURCE TO SEA

There Anne's influence might have ended but for the intervention of King George IV. He was a great fan of Scott's writing and he decided he must get first-hand experience of these noble subjects and, therefore, he would be the first British monarch to visit Scotland since 1650. He invited all the Highland chieftains and their clan followers to a grand parade in Edinburgh in August 1822. The pageant was overseen

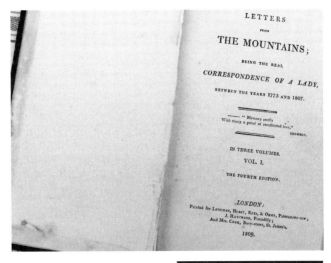

by Scott who was determined to persuade his fellow Scots that the King was just as much a Stuart as Bonnie Prince Charlie had been. He required not only Highland chieftains but Lowland gentlemen to turn up in full clan tartan. The request spread panic among both groups. Many clans had no specific designs and their chiefs hurriedly had to have new tartans made up to represent individual clans. And the Lowlanders had to search desperately for some Highland ancestry, however tenuous.

The King decided that Royal Stuart was 'his' tartan and spent the best part of £1,500 on the full outfit from George Hunter and Co. of Princes Street. The effect was somewhat spoiled by the flesh-coloured pantaloons he wore to conceal his bloated legs.

The parade was a huge success and Anne Grant, by now widowed and living in a flat overlooking Edinburgh's Royal Mile, watched it all from her window. Her son, the only survivor of her 12 children, was in the procession and I imagine her with a rueful smile as she noted the bizarre costumes that were the unintended outcome of her innocent letters from Laggan. There's nothing quite like a newly re-invented tradition, is there? So the next time you're at a wedding in Shetland, or the Borders or even London, and you see guests wearing the kilt – as they do, although they probably have no 'right' to wear it – you might remember Anne Grant and her unwitting role in the tartanification of Scotland.

Top:
Title page from *Letters from the Mountains*
Middle:
Sir Walter Scott by Sir Henry Raeburn
Scottish National Portrait Gallery
Bottom:
King George IV in full Highland costume by Sir David Wilkie
Royal Collection

Walk 1 – Dun na Lamh

Start: Cross the Spey just below the dam where a track goes off on the left.

Distance: 7 kms   Time: 2 hours   Grade: Strenuous

Follow the track for 500m, then take a forestry track on the right. After 1km turn right again for the slog to the summit of Dun na Lamh. You will, I promise, be impressed by the sheer size of the fortifications and, on a clear day, the view across the upper Spey valley to the Monadhliaths and the distant Cairngorms makes it all worthwhile.

Top:
Walk 1 – View from part way up Dun na Lamh across to Laggan and the Monadhliaths

Left:
Part of the fortifications at the summit of Dun na Lamh

Right:
Spey Dam

KIT HOUSES, 19th CENTURY STYLE

Buildings like this are still to be seen around the Highlands. The house above is about half a mile before you reach the village of Laggan. It's a house, obviously, but it's a kit house. In the late 19th and early 20th centuries if you were thinking of moving up in the world from an old-fashioned stone-built croft house, you could get a catalogue from firms like R. R. Speirs of Glasgow or William Cooper of London. They offered a range of designs with drawings to tempt the discerning buyer. What about the two-bedroom model, darling?

The kit would be despatched by boat or train and then onwards by horse and cart and you could either lay your own foundations and assemble the kit – the parts were numbered for ease of assembly – or the lads from the company could do that for you, for a few pounds extra.

And not just houses. Village schools, halls, churches, hospitals and club houses could all be ordered and were, according to the brochure, "suitable for all Climates". On a recent trip to New Zealand I was driving through a village in the North Island when I spotted a kit village hall. Fine examples of both church and school can be seen at the Folk Museum in Newtonmore (see Chapter Two)

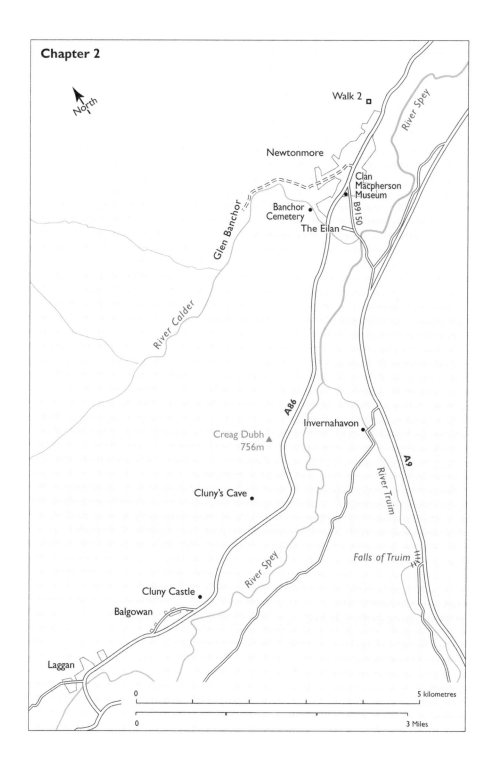

Chapter 2

North

Walk 2

Newtonmore

River Spey

Clan
Macpherson
Museum

Banchor
Cemetery

Glen Banchor

B9150

The Eilan

River Calder

A86

Invernahavon

Creag Dubh
756m

A9

River Truim

Cluny's Cave

Falls of Truim

River Spey

Cluny Castle

Balgowan

Laggan

0   5 kilometres

0   3 Miles

Chapter Two

Hooks and Hooligans

Laggan to Newtonmore

The parish of Laggan was blessed with two outstanding GPs. Dr Iain Richardson has chronicled the life and history of the parish (*Laggan: Past and Present*. Laggan Community Association 1990). And Dr Kenneth McKay was well known in piping circles and adjudicated at many piping competitions. He was also the doctor whose parish stretched to Newtonmore in an emergency and, on one occasion, I *was* such an emergency.

Laggan village store

As boys, my wee brother Brian and I were fishing the River Calder for trout and the occasional salmon parr, using worms and what we knew as Stewart tackle consisting of three hooks, with the middle hook at 180° to the other two. Perhaps they've ceased to exist because worm fishing is frowned upon, but they worked very well in Highland burns and rivers.

I was attaching a fresh worm when Brian walked past me on the riverbank, tripped over my line and caused one of the hooks to do to my thumb what it was intended to do to a trout's mouth. I yelped. Brian tried to extract the hook

Victim (Donald) on right, perpetrator (Brian) on left.

but the barb was having none of it. I yelped some more, so Brian cut the cast and we headed home, hook *in situ*. Even my mother couldn't get the hook out, so Dr McKay was called. With mother acting as anaesthetist – holding a pad of ether to my face – he quickly opened a little slit in my thumb and I was free.

So far, so mundane. It was what the good doctor did next that is the mark of the man. When he got back to his Laggan home, he examined the hook under a microscope and saw that the tip of the barb was missing. Next thing I knew I was in the Northern Infirmary in Inverness having the tiny but potentially lethal fragment removed. I was presented with the offending fragment and kept it for many years in a match box. But it is thanks to Dr McKay's conscientiousness that my thumb – with a faint 55 year-old scar – is still with me.

Half a mile along the Newtonmore road from Dr McKay's house is Cluny Castle. Not so much a castle, more a fine Georgian mansion, it used to be the seat of the Clan Macpherson. Queen Victoria and Prince Albert looked at two other Highland hideaways before they settled on Balmoral. One was Ardverikie Lodge on Loch Laggan, better known as Glenbogle in the BBC's *Monarch of the Glen*. The other was Cluny Castle. How Laggan's fortunes might have been

transformed, although whether for better or worse is hard to say. For myself, I like it fine the way it is.

The chief of the Clan Macpherson is always called Cluny and the chief in 1745 fought alongside Charles Edward Stuart – and paid the price. The original Cluny Castle was destroyed by Government troops and Cluny himself joined other Jacobites on the run. He spent several years hiding out on his estate and, in particular, in a cave perched precariously amongst the cliffs of Creag Dubh, the mountain which stands between Laggan and Newtonmore. He lived partly from supplies delivered to him by local sympathisers and, according to legend, on the meat from a herd of wild goats. The chief finally escaped to France where he died in 1756.

Before attempting to reach the cave recently I asked locally if the herd still survived. I was told confidently that they had long since died out. But in the rocks below the cliffs I came across a wild nanny with her kid and even managed to snatch a very poor photograph. A little later I met a proper photographer who had been taking photographs of a spectacular 100ft waterfall nearby. He wondered what its name was and I had to tell him it didn't have a name for the simple reason that it only appears a few days each year after heavy rain. But, as consolation, I told him about the goats and I was gratified to see some photographs of the herd in a later edition of the *Scottish Field*. If he reads this, the photographer knows where to send the usual fee!

As youngsters, my older brother Norman, Brian and I used to climb up to the famous cave – without parental approval, obviously – and it came as a painful reality check that on this recent occasion I chickened out. All the more galling because, along with a group of fellow students from the Royal Scottish Academy of Music – all keen climbers – I'd spotted some very promising-looking routes on Creag Dubh which, according to the climbing guidebooks, had never been climbed before. We kept the information to ourselves and planned to tackle the

'Extinct' goats

routes at a later date and, what's more, to exercise our right as first ascenders to name the routes after Scottish composers. Sadly – for us and for Scottish music – we were beaten to it by the famous Dougal Haston and the Edinburgh Squirrels who polished off most of the routes in two weekends in 1962. I think we have a glimmer of where their minds were at the time by the names they gave the routes, now preserved for posterity in the climbing guidebooks – Cunnilinctus, Phellatio and Tongue Twister. Hooligans!

Cluny's cave – it's there somewhere above the black streaks

More recently, I decided I really needed a photograph showing I could still make it to the cave, but local enquiries revealed a rockfall had made an already perilous approach even more dangerous and, in any case, the cairn marking the start of the traverse to the cave has disappeared. Perhaps I'll have managed it by the next edition!

Directly across the Spey from Creag Dubh is the site of the Battle of Invernahavon, 1386, which ended in victory for the Clan Chattan – including Macphersons and Macintoshes[1]

---

[1] The spelling of names starting with Mc or Mac can be troublesome. In the case of Macpherson, the clan uses this form, but some individuals use or used MacPherson and where we know of this, we are happy to oblige.

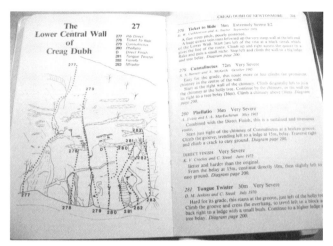

Evidence of hooliganism from: *Rock and Ice Climbs, Lochaber and Badenoch*, SMC 1981

as well as Cattanachs and Davidsons – over the Lochaber Camerons. Mind you, a battle between rival clans in Scotland puts me in mind of the legendary headline 'Earthquake in Chile – few casualties' and it seems appropriate that the site of the battle is now a caravan park.

But if the Battle of Invernahavon isn't the most exciting piece of Scottish history, it's a lot more exciting than the mountain that distantly overlooks the site of the battle. Meall na Cuaich is a strong contender to be Scotland's most boring mountain – a great, featureless lump at the north end of the Drumochter hills (themselves close runners-up in the boring mountain stakes!). The long trek in to reach Meall na Cuaich means the mountain would ordinarily be given a wide berth by hill walkers. But for one thing. It is just over 3,000ft high and, therefore, is compulsory for that single-minded – or possibly obsessive-compulsive – group, the Munro baggers, determined to scale all 284 mountains in Scotland over 3,000ft. They have to set aside a whole day to slog up its heathery, boggy slopes.

Some years ago I was talking to a prominent member of the Scottish Mountaineering Club in a bar in Edinburgh and somehow the subject of Meall na Cuaich cropped up. He swore to me that he'd left enough money in his will to hire a JCB to scalp the mountain down to 2,999ft and thereby save a lot of people a lot of drudgery. Maybe he was lying, or maybe he's still alive and well,

Scotland's answer to the Matterhorn (not) Meall na Cuaich

but nothing's happened yet. But I can see the movie now, with Hugh Grant in a nice piece of role reversal (for those who missed it, the film is called *The Englishman who went up a hill and came down a mountain*).

The village of Newtonmore was established in the mid 19th century by crofters forced out of nearby Glen Banchor to make way for more profitable sheep as part of the Highland Clearances. Truth to tell, although in summer sunshine Glen Banchor is a lovely place, it can be also be pretty bleak. Standing on a freezing winter's day surveying the sad piles of stones marking all that remains of the crofting townships, it's hard to be convinced that crofting had much of a future hereabouts, even without the intervention of hard-nosed landowners. The land is thin and sour, the wind howls down the glen. It must have been a brutally hard life. That may sound like treachery to the people who were evicted, but since one of them was my great-grandfather, Donald Cattanach, I feel entitled to tell it like I see it. Be that as it may, Donald and the other families were forced to start a new life in the village down by the Spey, and I shall come back to him in the next chapter.

The Cattanachs are – depending on which version of clan history you choose – either a small sept of the larger Clan Macpherson or they are the originals. The name derives from the Pictish Catii tribe, greatly feared by the Romans. You may not be altogether surprised to hear that my vote goes to the latter version. But whichever version is true, we are now in the heartland of the clan, which is why so many of the characters in this, and the next, part of the Spey story are Macphersons. In fact, the more modern use of Clan Chattan is as a federation of several clans, the most prominent being the Macphersons and the Macintoshes.

Approaching Newtonmore from Laggan and just after crossing the River Calder, you will see on the left an intriguing sign in Gaelic pointing to the Banchor Cemetery. The sign was erected as part of the settlement of an important court case in 1878 between the local people and the landowner, who had

blocked the access road with a new steading. The Court of Session in Edinburgh found in favour of the locals and re-

Top left:
Clan Macpherson gathering

Top right:
Sign required by law

Left:
Newtonmore Main Street with Creag Dubh

Right:
Clan Macpherson Musuem, aka Glenbogle Tearoom

quired the owner not only to re-open the path but to pay for the sign to be erected.

One of many examples of local landmarks adopting different personae since the advent of *Monarch of the Glen* was the Clan Macpherson Museum which turned into the Glenbogle Tearoom and Post Office. I don't recommend trying to post a letter at the museum these days!

Since most of the other towns and villages in Badenoch and Strathspey also claim a connection with the series, this will be the last mention of *Monarch of the Glen*. Probably.

Walk 2 – Newtonmore

Newtonmore is hard to beat for the number and variety of walks in and around the village. A dozen or so are in a well-illustrated folder produced by the Wildcat Centre beside the village hall. Here is one of them.

> *Start: At the east end of Main Street is Strone Road. A short way up, at the Water Authority sign, is a small car park.*

Distance: 5 kms   Time: About an hour   Grade: Moderate

Ahead you can admire the great arch of the Monadhliath Mountains from Creag Dhu to Creag Bheag. Cross the burn by the wooden bridge and from now on the route is well signposted. The boulders strewn around are the remains of the crofting township of Strone and there is a plaque detailing the original layout of the settlement as well as naming the distant hills. Look behind you at the marvellous view across Strathspey to the Glen Feshie Cairngorms.

To the left is a series of waterfalls and the track leads on down to some mixed woodland and arrives back at a lay-by on the old A9 and from there through a conifer wood back to Strone Road and up to the car park (if you are on foot, there's no need to go up to the car park!)

The burn, by the way, is the Allt Laraidh and the pool beside the lay-by held a momentous significance once upon a time. That's where Brian and I, as wee boys, had our first success fishing. We caught two, but they were eels and it's the very devil to get the hook out of them. One went to a group of hungry German hitch hikers who were very impressed. The other, hanging from the handlebars, went back home with us for Aunt Bainie to cook for our tea.

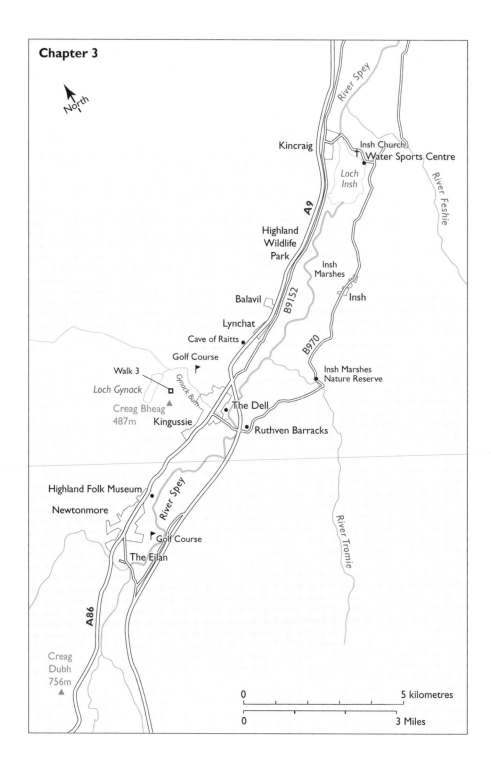

Chapter 3

North

Kincraig
Insh Church
Water Sports Centre

Loch Insh

A9

River Spey

River Feshie

Highland Wildlife Park

Insh Marshes

B9152

Balavil

Insh

Lynchat

Cave of Raitts

B970

Golf Course

Walk 3

Insh Marshes Nature Reserve

Gynack Burn

Loch Gynack

Creag Bheag
487m

The Dell

Kingussie

Ruthven Barracks

Highland Folk Museum

River Spey

Newtonmore

Golf Course

River Tromie

The Eilan

A86

Creag Dubh
756m

0   5 kilometres

0   3 Miles

Chapter Three

Shinty and Scallywags

Newtonmore to Kincraig

Let's talk about local rivalries for a moment. You know the kind of thing – Glasgow/Edinburgh, Rangers/Celtic, Scotland/England. The best rivalries require love *and* hate, private respect and public scorn; the best rivals always have more in common than they care to admit. Take Newtonmore and Kingussie then. Two villages – or perhaps a village and a town – separated by just three miles, populations either side of a thousand souls each, both pretty, bustling communities set in wonderful scenery.

But when it comes to shinty, the rivalry could not be fiercer.

For many years, Newtonmore won everything in sight. Then in the 1980s and 90s Kingussie became – according to the *Guinness Book of World Records* – the world's most successful sporting team of all time, winning 20 consecutive league titles and going four seasons without losing a game. If they have faltered somewhat in recent years, they have still won the league more often than any other team since 2000. (See Appendix Three p115)

Approaching Newtonmore from the south, the road – the old A9 now called the A86 – crosses the Spey and as it sweeps round towards the village, the Eilan – Newtonmore's shinty ground – is on the left. The size of the pitch gives a hint at what a fast, ferocious and energy-sapping game this is. It has been called clan warfare with a referee and injuries caused by camans (shinty sticks) meeting flesh and bone are frequent and spectacular. The Eilan is also the venue for the annual Newtonmore Highland Games, one of the oldest in the Highlands.

The Games coincide with the annual gathering of the Clan Macpherson when the men of the clan march behind their chief and local and visiting pipe bands in the shadow of Creag Dubh, which is not only the traditional war-cry of the clan but is also the site of the annual hill race.

Away from the shinty pitch, Newtonmore is a Highland village which thrives on tourism. On offer are golf and tennis, bowling and fishing and an impressive range of walks, from evening strolls to serious expeditions. It also boasts the

Clan warfare with sticks instead of swords. Kingussie's record goal-scorer Ronald Ross with helmet

unique Waltzing Waters, a display of fountains with multi-coloured lighting and music.

Newtonmore is also the site of the highly successful Highland Folk Museum. The museum started life in Kingussie just after World War II as a living museum of Highland life, including a blackhouse, claimed to be Britain's oldest recreated building. In 1995 Turus Tim, a mile-long site at Newtonmore, was opened including an 18th century township and a 1940s farm with working demonstrations and local people acting as live interpreters.

On a recent visit to the site we came across a small group of local students in the reconstructed classroom tasting the delights of slates and inkwells

Top
Newtonmore Highland Games

Middle
Kit school

Bottom
Ink-stained classroom

and trying to write with a scratchy school pen without either creating a page full of blots or covering fingers in blue-black stains. And the school building itself is another example of a kit, assembled on the spot from prefabricated sections (see Chapter One).

There is another museum in Newtonmore – the Clan Macpherson Museum – and if I tell you that two of their prize exhibits are a broken violin and

the workings of an old clock, you may be somewhat underwhelmed. But wait, this is no ordinary knackered fiddle. It belonged to one James MacPherson. And the old clock played a crucial part in the story.

Back in the late 17th century, MacPherson was a famous – perhaps notorious is the word – freebooter, highwayman, fiddler, singer, storyteller and womaniser. It was said at the time that wherever James MacPherson was, there was a ceilidh. The authorities, though, took a dim view of his wealth redistribution activities and tried repeatedly to lay hands on

The broken fiddle in the Clan Macpherson Museum

him, but were always thwarted because the local population – and especially the womenfolk – were only too willing to offer him a safe haven when things became sticky.

So the authorities came up with a cunning plan. At the annual fair in the town of Keith, they arranged for an attractive young woman to befriend the bold James. She invited him back for a cup of tea – or whatever – and they were in the middle of 'whatever' when his pursuers burst in and captured him without resistance and in a state of *déshabillé*, as they say in polite circles. He was tried and sentenced to hang, despite the fact that his long criminal career had never involved much in the way of violence. He appealed against the sentence and the case was heard in Edinburgh just days before he was due to be hanged in the town square in Banff in 1700. The appeal was granted and a letter of reprieve was prepared and sent by messenger on horseback.

Keith Show, where the bold James was entrapped

**Clock workings
for a doomed man**

But news of the impending reprieve reached Banff before the messenger did, and one of the town councillors arranged for the town hall clock to be moved forward by an hour. Meanwhile, beneath the gallows, MacPherson was entertaining the crowd with a last tune and as the hour of execution approached, he offered his fiddle to the spectators. No one dared accept the gift so he broke the instrument over his knee and was duly hanged.

They say his body was still twitching as the official messenger came clattering over the Brig o' Banff bearing the reprieve, but that could be a later ornamentation to the story. What is probably authentic is the fiddle in the Clan Macpherson museum. And the other key object in the drama – the town hall clock – stopped keeping time and the story goes that the clock was going to be scrapped by Banff's council. The councillors in nearby Dufftown asked for it, repaired it, and it kept time in the clock tower in the square until it was re-placed by the present electric clock. The original workings have now found their final resting place in the Museum.

And the last word on James MacPherson concerns the tune he played on the gallows. It was written down soon after and is one of Scotland's oldest pub-lished fiddle tunes. Robert Burns later put words to the tune and it is now known as either MacPherson's Farewell or MacPherson's Rant.

MACPHERSON'S RANT

Farewell, ye dungeons dark and strong,
The wretch's destinie!
MacPherson's time will not be long
On yonder gallows-tree.

Sae rantingly, sae wantonly,
Sae dauntingly gaed he,
He play'd a spring, and danc'd it round
Below the gallows-tree.

J. Macpherson

With Vigour ♩ = 120

BURNS

[Fine]

boldly

Da Capo

Sae rantingly, sae wantonly,
Sae dauntingly gaed he,
He play'd a spring, and danc'd it round
Below the gallows-tree.

Farewell, ye dungeons dark and strong,
The wretch's destinie!
MacPherson's time will no be long
Below the gallows-tree.

Macpherson's Rant

Dufftown clock tower

Both Newtonmore and Kingussie are now by-passed by the A9 on the opposite (eastern) side of the Spey, but the old road still connects the two communities. There used to be a rather famous inn at Pitmain on the outskirts of Kingussie, and in 1838 one Amelia Stuart-Menzie and her brother the Rev Alexander Irvine stayed at the inn during an arduous journey through Badenoch. The Rev was

Typical Kingussie Victorian villa

not exactly delighted and reckoned Pitmain was 'the worst and dirtiest Inn on the north road'.

Whereas Newtonmore can only trace its origins back to the middle of the 19th century, Kingussie's history goes back a long way. A chapel, dedicated to St Columba, was founded here in 565 AD. But its modern history really starts in the late 18th century when the existing hamlet was expanded under the direction of the Duke of Gordon. And then the railway arrived in 1863, coinciding with the blossoming passion by well-to-do Victorians for all things Highland. They came for the huntin', shootin' and fishin' and built large villas which still give the place ideas of grandeur over the other villages – and especially Newtonmore. Kingussie even claims to be the only town in Badenoch, having been made a police burgh in 1867.

Bird hide at Insh Marshes Nature Reserve

Like its neighbours, Kingussie's economy depends heavily on tourism and it offers visitors a wide range of outdoor activities. There are golf courses

in most of the towns and villages in this book, (see Appendix One) all with their own character. In the case of Kingussie, the course is rolling parkland with spectacular views and the 15th hole is a particular favourite, played from one side of the River Gynack to the other.

Ruthven
Barracks

Just east of Kingussie, the RSPB's Insh Marshes Nature Reserve is one of Europe's most important areas of flood plain wetland, where large numbers of waterfowl breed or spend the winter months. Species include redshanks and curlews and, in winter, whooper swans and greylag geese. There are hides and nature trails and guided tours during the summer months.

Heading out of the village towards the impressive Ruthven Barracks is Kingussie's shinty ground, the Dell. But it is the barracks that draw the eye. They stand on a mound that is partly man-made and dominates the surrounding area. The first fortification was built in the 13th century by the Comyn Earls of Badenoch and it was destroyed by the Jacobites during the 1689 rising. Following the next uprising in 1715, General Wade built the present barracks as part of his pacification of the Highlands. And, following the disaster at Culloden in 1746, the Jacobites gathered at Ruthven to receive their commander's order to disperse. The long years of Jacobite uprisings were over.

There was, however, a previous occupant of the mound, the infamous

**Wolf of Badenoch's tomb
in Dunkeld Cathedral**
image from itravel.com

The Wolf's handiwork:
the remains of
Elgin Cathedral

Alexander Stewart, 1st Earl of Buchan, better known as the Wolf of Badenoch. I think it would be fair to say his nickname was well-earned. He married the Countess of Ross in 1382. The marriage produced no children and Alexander blamed his wife – as men are wont to do – only this time he might have had a case. Alexander was well on his way to fathering around 40 illegitimate children, so there didn't seem to be much wrong on his side of the bed, so to speak.

But Alexander was not happy about the absence of a legitimate heir and he asked the Bishop of Moray to annul the marriage. The bishop sided with the countess who still found herself thrown out to make way for Alexander's latest mistress. Blithely unaware of what was coming his way, the bishop promptly excommunicated the earl who set about earning his unofficial title.

The monk who delivered news of the excommunication was thrown into a bottle pit in Lochindorb Castle – one of the Wolf's many Highland lairs – and then Alexander set about his revenge. And how! He attacked Moray with a large band of his ferocious henchmen, sacked the town of Forres, destroyed Pluscarden Abbey and, as the *coup de grâce*, reduced Elgin Cathedral – the second largest in Scotland – and its associated hospital the Maison Dieu, to the ruin it is today.

But never let it be said that evil men do not receive their comeuppance. Four years after his assault on Moray, the Wolf retired to Ruthven Castle which stood on the site of Ruthven Barracks. On the night of 24 July 1394, a stranger dressed all in black arrived at the door of the castle and challenged him to a

game of chess. They were well-matched and, by the light of guttering candles and with a violent thunderstorm in the background (as they say in all the best ghost stories), the game continued long into the night.

Finally the dark stranger called 'Check Mate!', there was a crash of thunder and, in the morning, the castle servants were found outside the walls, apparently killed by lightning. And the Wolf himself lay dead in the castle, without a mark on him, but all the nails had been torn out of his boots and lay scattered on the floor – or so they say.

Back on the A9, just north of Kingussie, the Ordnance Survey marks a souterrain. It is better known as the Cave of Raitts and was long thought to be a remarkable natural phenomenon. But more recently it has been established that it is man-made and probably dates from the Bronze Age. It is about 80ft long and eight feet high and, although it might have been used to store surplus food in a cool space, its purpose is not really understood. But there's a story – of course!

Back in the good old days of clan warfare, the McNivens and Macphersons were having a bit of a feud and the Macphersons were puzzled that their rivals could mount raids and then disappear into thin air. Cluny Macpherson ordered his son to find out what was going on, and he narrowed his search to the hills just north of Kingussie.

Exhausted by a day on horseback, he sought shelter for the night in a

Balavil House aka Kilwillie Castle

small lean-to occupied by two elderly women. They refused his request, a serious and suspicious breach of the norms of Highland hospitality. The son left, but – certain that something fishy was going on – came back and demanded to be allowed to sleep in a corner. Through half-closed eyes he watched one of the women place a tray of freshly-baked scones in a press in the back wall of the little house.

A short while later, she repeated the process and he saw that the first scones had vanished. He said nothing, left early the next morning and summoned a well-armed group of his clansmen. He finally dealt with the McNivens who had, of course, been using the cave behind the lean-to as a base for their operations.

James 'Ossian' Macpherson

Less than a mile past the Cave of Raitts is Balavil, an impressive country house which has been in Macpherson hands since it was built in 1790 by James 'Ossian' Macpherson. Balavil was the setting for Killwillie Castle in the BBC television series *Monarch of the Glen*. (Sorry!)

But it is James 'Ossian' Macpherson who has left the more lasting legacy. He was born in Ruthven and went to university in Aberdeen. In the mid 18th century he produced a stream of books purporting to be translations of ancient Gaelic texts, the most famous of which was *Fingal*, a series of epic poems in the style of Homer, supposedly written by Fingal's son Ossian. The book was a tremendous success; it was translated into many languages and took Europe by storm. Goethe incorporated part of the epic in his *The*

44

Sorrows of Young Werther, and an Italian translation was one of Napoleon's favourite books.

There were sceptics, however, who doubted the authenticity, if not the quality, of Macpherson's work, and the leading doubter was Dr Samuel Johnson who asserted that the works were largely Macpherson's own re-working of fragments of ancient Gaelic writings.

It is now thought that Johnson's scepticism was probably well-founded and Macpherson never produced the original writings that would have proved his case. But at the height of his popularity, the impressive cave on the island of Staffa was renamed Fingal's Cave and, inspired by a visit to the island, Mendelssohn wrote the famous overture of the same name.

Macpherson returned to his native Badenoch and saw out his days in Balavil House, earning a reputation as a good landlord when such people were few and far between.

If you want a vivid impression of the natural fauna of the Highlands as it once was, a visit to the Highland Wildlife Park, another mile north on the A9, will be rewarding. The park boasts an impressive range of animals and birds, some still native to Scotland but endangered, others – like the European bison – extinct except for those in captivity. Visitors can drive round much of the park but there are also walk-round areas. Walkers and cyclists can be driven by park staff.

Just beyond the park is the village of Kincraig. Across the bridge from the

Insh Church

village, in a copse where Loch Insh returns to being the River Spey, is the ancient white-washed Insh Church. Like so many churches throughout Scotland, in 1843 it became embroiled in the Disruption. The Presbyterian Church of Scotland had, since the Union of the Parliaments of England and Scotland in 1707, come under increasing pressure to come into line with the Church of England with its hierarchy of archbishops at the top and vicars appointed by the local landowner at ground level. It was also put under pressure to accept that, as an established church, it owed sovereignty to the state rather than to God.

At a General Assembly in Edinburgh, a third of Scotland's ministers and congregations determined, amongst other things, to maintain their traditional right to have ministers elected by all the members of a church. They broke away to form the Free Church.

At Insh Church, 25 members of the congregation walked out. Gathering on a hillock in the village of Insh a mile away they considered their options. No minister, no church building, no money. A majority of those who had broken away were likely to have been former crofters who had been cleared out of Glenfeshie, so it is hardly surprising that they wanted nothing to do with landowners appointing their spiritual leaders.

But they did remember that there were others in a similar position, including Donald Cattanach at Newtonmore, a crofter/mason and part-time lay preacher and, most relevantly, a cleared crofter like themselves. And, despite the 16-mile round trip on foot, Donald Cattanach became their unpaid minister for many years.

The immediate problem of the lack of a church building was overcome by one of the women in the congregation weaving a plaid to protect him – and the Holy Book – from the elements. The plaid was passed down through the generations and ended up, faded and threadbare, on top of my wardrobe. It has now found a much better home in the Highland Folk Museum.

Donald Cattanach, you will have worked out, was my great grandfather.

Donald Cattanach
in the late 1880s

The shawl finds a better
home

The Strathspey and Badenoch Herald

Family heirloom finds new home in museum

A FAMILY with its roots steeped in Badenoch history presented a 150-year-old family heirloom to the Kingussie branch of the Highland Folk Museum last week.

The shawl, or plaid, belonged to Mr Donald Barr's father and his father before him. It has been passed down the line in a bid to keep the family history alive.

Mr Barr, a member of the Cattanach clan from Newtonmore, and his seven-month-old grandson – Callum Cattanach Barr – can now see it preserved for posterity in a place which can also explain to visitors and locals alike, the ecclesiastical history behind it.

Donald's grandfather, Donald Cattanach, had been given the plaid by his Free Church congregation, who had made it for him to ward off the elements when he preached in the open air at a time before a church building existed.

Donald has been waiting for some time to get his family together to officially present the plaid to the museum, so that they could preserve it and teach others about their own history.

Donald's brother Brian travelled from London and

By ANDREA ELDERFIELD

around 1840 to the new adjoining, and more sheltered, town on the moor – Newtonmore.

The first house, Craigellachie, had been built around 1780 by an earlier Cattanach.

In 1843 a historical landmark in the history of Scottish churches occurred when 190 ministers walked out of the General Assembly in Edinburgh to create their own church – The Free Church of Scotland.

At Insh, with its ancient and small congregation, a similar turmoil took place and 20 of the congregation walked out of the established church, although they didn't have a building to worship in, no minister and no money to employ one.

"The most urgent problem was to find someone with education and a knowledge of the Bible who would do it for nothing or next to nothing. A fully trained minister was completely out of the question," said Donald.

"Somebody mentioned Donald Cattanach, the Catechist from Newton-

to preach to his flock. After some time they managed to build a 'wee mission house', but until then they held their services in the open air.

"By way of protection

Donald Barr shows off the historic plaid, helped by Mr Ross Noble, right, curator of the Highland folk Museum, to his two sons Douglas and Alasdair, brother Brian and grandson Callum Cattanach Barr.

to be pointed out to us as youngsters," explained Mr Barr, who was brought up in Glasgow, but now lives in Keith.

The plaid will remain at the Kingussie museum for

they could not accept it.

"They have got more space now," said Mr Barr. "I am just absolutely delighted that the museum is going to make the display and I hope

church that kept Gaelic going when it was not even taught in the schools and I am very pleased to be able to contribute something to the history," said Mr Barr.

Highlands during that time.

"The fact that the people gave a plaid to an open air preacher is very significant factor coming from people who were not very well off.

SHINTY AND SCALLYWAGS

47

Creag Bheag

Walk 3 – Above Kingussie

This walk takes you to the top of Creag Bheag. Now you may know that 'bheag' means 'small' in Gaelic, but this is a small mountain, not a hill. The walk is circular.

> *Start: The car park at the caravan site below the golf course*
>
> *Distance: About 6kms*
>
> *Time: About two-and-a-half hours*
>
> *Grade: Strenuous*

From the car park, cross the road and go through a gate which takes you through part of the caravan site and into mixed woods of birch, hazel and pine. You are following signs to Creag Bheag and Golf Course circular. The latter is a gentler alternative and takes a bit over an hour. In sight of Loch Gynack the routes part company.

This is the most strenuous part of the walk and is a simple slog to the top of Creag Bheag. The mountain has several summits, the official one having a welcome bench protected by a dry-stane windbreak. The path then leaves the summit ridge and down past some crags to the forest plantation. Here there is a choice. Left is the direct route, right a more leisurely alternative, but both end at West Terrace. Turn left, admiring the Victorian mansions, back to the golf course road and turn left, back up to the starting point.

If the weather is kind you will have had some wonderful views over Kingussie to the Glen Feshie Cairngorms.

LIFE'S A BEACH AT LOCH INSH

The Loch Insh Water Sports Centre was founded by a man with a name so fitting even I couldn't make it up! Clive Freshwater came to public attention with a campaign to establish the right of canoeists to navigate the River Spey. The centre now offers a huge range of sporting activity, from the original canoeing to dinghy sailing, windsurfing, archery, mountain biking and walking as well as winter sports.

In the early days of the centre, I visited with a geologist friend. As I was talking to Clive, my friend went to take a closer look at the fine little beach beside the centre. He asked to borrow a shovel and dug into the sand, becoming more and more excited with what he found.

'Forget your water sports centre,' he told a startled Clive. 'Build a big hotel and you'll get geologists from all over the world beating a path to your door. What you've got here is an inverted beach and the only other one I've heard of in the world is in Tasmania.'

An inverted beach, he explained, is where the material on top is a lot older than the material underneath. At some point a great geological upheaval has, in effect, turned the beach upside down.

'I promise you,' my friend went on, 'Geologists will be coming here with their students from all over the world.'

'Really?' said Clive.

'Yes, really.'

'And will they still come if they find out I laid the beach a couple of years ago with 25 lorry loads of sand from the quarry up the road?'

'Ah... right.'

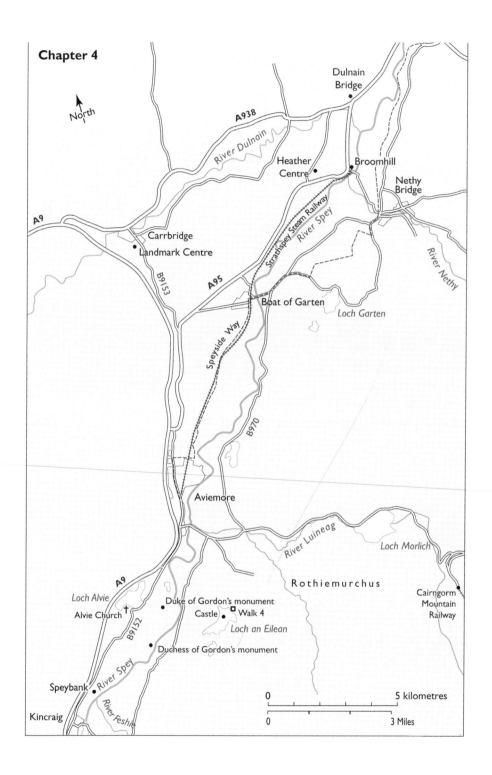

North

Dulnain
Bridge

A938

River Dulnain

Heather
Centre

Broomhill

Nethy
Bridge

Strathspey Steam Railway

River Spey

River Nethy

A9

Carrbridge

Landmark Centre

B9153

A95

Boat of Garten

Loch Garten

Speyside Way

B970

Aviemore

River Luineag

Loch Morlich

Rothiemurchus

A9

Loch Alvie

Duke of Gordon's monument

Cairngorm
Mountain
Railway

Alvie Church †

Castle ● □ Walk 4

B9152

Loch an Eilean

Duchess of Gordon's monument

Speybank

River Spey

Kincraig

River Feshie

0   5 kilometres

0   3 Miles

Chapter Four

Ospreys and a Plethora of Bridges

Kincraig to Nethybridge

Just after the village of Kincraig, the River Feshie joins the Spey at Speybank and there is a fine walk from the village to the junction of the rivers. Further on the Spey sweeps on past Loch Alvie, and overlooking the loch is Alvie Church. The

first record of a chapel on the site dates from 1380, but when they were renovating the ancient church in 1880, the builders made a gruesome discovery.

The traditional cobbled floor was being replaced with wooden boards and 150 skeletons were found, buried head-to-head. Researchers concluded they were killed in battle, although no weapons were found with them.

The bones were re-interred in the church's cemetery under the legend:

Alvie Church

> Buried here are the Remains of 150 Human Bodies Found, October
> 1880, beneath the Floor of this Church. Who they were, When they
> lived, How they Died, Tradition Notes not. Their Bones are Dust,
> Their good Swords Rust, their souls are with the Saints we Trust.

Memorial to the
Duchess of Gordon

On the opposite side of the Spey is a small wooded hill with 'his and hers'

monuments at either end. To the south is the modest memorial to the Duchess of Gordon half-hidden amongst foliage and tricky to find, while the Duke's is a remarkably phallic edifice dominating the surrounding lands. Were 'his and hers' not ever thus?

About a mile south east of the Duke's monument is the beautiful Loch an Eilean, named after the island on which there is a 13th century castle which

became one of the Wolf of Badenoch's favourite holiday hideaways. This is a perfect spot to savour the smells and atmosphere of the Caledonian pine forests, and a path runs around the loch; the castle very probably comes second only to Eilean Donan Castle in the most-photographed stakes. I have been unable to confirm the information that the last osprey to be shot in Scotland met its maker at Loch an Eilean.

And then comes Aviemore, tourist capital of Badenoch and Strathspey. I think it would be

fair to say that Aviemore has had a pretty topsy-turvy time in the post-war years. I can remember it as one of the smallest of the Badenoch villages, its only feature the fact that it was a railway junction. I can still hear the ghostly voice of the stationmaster announcing 'Aviemore Junction, Aviemore Junction. Change here for Keith Junction'. Sadly, thanks to Dr Beeching and his redrawing

of the railway map of Britain in the 1960s, two of the three lines running north of Aviemore are as ghostly as the voice (or nearly so – see Strathspey Railway below).

At the same time as the lines were disappearing, the Scottish skiing industry was starting to develop. Aviemore was the nearest settlement to the Cairngorms. It still had the Perth to Inverness railway and

Aviemore station

in 1964 the Aviemore Centre appeared, thanks to the vision of Sir Hugh Fraser. Not everyone thought the centre was altogether wonderful. The architecture was not to everyone's taste and in its early years it felt rather bleak and ill-at-ease set amongst the grandeur of the mountains. The centre has improved recently, but Aviemore lives with the uncertain future of Scottish skiing.

Ill-at-ease? MacDonald Hotel, Aviemore

At the risk of stating the blindingly obvious, the Cairngorms are not the Alps. Although they are 2,000 miles to the north, at their highest the Cairngorms are barely a third of the height of many Alpine peaks. The terrain is more Arctic than Alpine and so is the weather. Wind, especially, used to make skiing impossible on around 40 per cent of winter days. So skiing in Scotland was always a marginal proposition.

Downhill skiing. Going downhill?

My brother, Brian, who learned his skiing in Scotland, recalls his first visit to the Alps. On the first morning it was grey and windy, with steady snowfall. A few lifts were operating and he was surprised to find himself alone going up the

first tow. As he skied back down, still alone, another figure emerged from the gloom. They stopped to have a chat. He turned out to be another Scot, and they agreed it wasn't at all a bad day to be on the hill and where was everyone else?

But global warming is taking its toll. Aviemore may have to learn to live without downhill skiing at least, although the Cairngorm Mountain Railway, opened to much controversy in

2001, has made the main skiing area accessible in winds that would have stopped the old tows in their tracks. The controversy was over the damage the railway would do to the fragile ecology of the high mountains, and a rule has been imposed preventing summer users of the railway from leaving the Ptarmigan top station. If you want to get to the top of Cairngorm, you have to go on foot from the bottom station.

Aviemore has another railway – the Strathspey Railway – using the old line from Aviemore to Boat of Garten and on to the village of Broomhill – which recreates the atmosphere of steam train travel in the 50s and 60s. In fact, the line was only closed for 10 years – from 1968 until the enthusiasts who bought the line re-opened it in 1978. There are plans to extend the railway to Grantown-on-Spey.

First stop on the Strathspey Railway is Boat of Garten, named – as you might expect – after a ferry that crossed the Spey at the village of Gart. Boat of Garten promotes itself as The Osprey Village, because a pair of these wonderful birds first returned to Scotland in 1954 to nest at nearby Loch Garten.

It is not certain exactly when ospreys died out in Scotland, but the last

Strathspey Railway loco takes on water at Boat of Garten

An osprey posing
with catch

breeding pair was recorded in 1916. In the mid 19th century, when egg-collecting was regarded as a perfectly proper pursuit, osprey eggs were highly prized.

The lengths to which a collector would go are illustrated by one Lewis Dunbar who, according to *Collins Encyclopaedia of Scotland*, robbed an osprey nest in the castle on Loch an Eilean five years in succession.

> In 1851 [he] arrived [at the loch] at 3am in a snowstorm after a 20-mile hike. Undeterred, the doughty Dunbar swam to the island, removed two eggs, and returned by swimming on his back with a egg in each hand; he then blew the eggs and rinsed them out with whisky before cheerfully hiking back to Grantown with his valuable prize and an excellent yarn.

I vividly recall the thrill I felt seeing that first pair at Loch Garten on and around their nest from the RSPB hide in the mid-1950s and, although I still get excited when I see an osprey, it doesn't quite match my admiration for those two adventurous birds who led the way back to Scotland.

I'm getting ahead of myself geographically, but I recently watched an adult osprey pick up a large salmon from the sea at Spey Bay. The fish was clearly meant for a nest of growing youngsters, but the bird struggled to get airborne and only just managed to reach land before dropping the salmon. The bird flew around for a few minutes before returning to the fish and giving it another try.

Loch Garten – scene of the osprey's return to Scotland

After 100 yards it had to drop it again. To hell with this, the bird seemed to say, and settled down to eat the salmon itself.

It has been a slow process, helping the osprey to re-establish itself in Scotland. Bad weather, nest robbers and clumsy accidents have taken their toll, but it is thought that, thanks to prodigious efforts by the RSPB and others, around 200 breeding pairs are now spread around the Highlands, although young birds have a habit of returning to nest very close to their parents. A bit like humans, really.

Oldest of Carrbridge's bridges – the Old Packhorse

The RSPB has a visitor centre at Loch Garten with hides and live camera links from the nest so that visitors can watch ospreys on the nest and hunting. There are also forest walks around the loch and a gift shop at the visitor centre which is open from April to August.

Boat of Garten has also become a way station on the Speyside Way which runs from

THE SPEY: FROM SOURCE TO SEA

Aviemore to Buckie on the Moray coast and this last section of the way runs alongside the steam railway track.

Now here's a question. How many bridges does one small village need? One to take the main road over the river. Check. One to take the railway over the river. Check. And maybe a pretty old bridge to give the place a bit of atmosphere. Check. So how come Carrbridge boasts no less than six bridges, all crossing the River Dulnain?

Going upstream, there is the bridge in the village that used to carry the old A9. Then there is the old Packhorse Bridge, built in 1717 following, according to local legend, a nasty incident involving a funeral party making their way to the cemetery on the far side of the Dulnain. The river was in spate, one of the pall bearers slipped and the coffin was dropped into the swollen river and never seen again, giving a whole extra meaning to the phrase 'dearly departed'.

Then there is the Ellan Bridge, built by a party of Ghurkhas in 1992. Then there is the bridge carrying the Perth-Inverness railway, then the new A9 bridge and finally the Sluggan Bridge, designed by Thomas Telford and built in the 1830s to replace a Wade bridge swept away in the Muckle Spate of 1829.

One small village, six bridges. I think it should be called 'Carrbridges'.

Although much of the population of Carrbridge are incomers – or do I mean 'Because…'? – the village is a lively wee place. And like many of the villages along the Spey, it has an attractive community website (a list of some of the best websites is at the end of this book).

Top
Old A9 bridge

Middle
Gurkha bridge, aka Ellan Bridge

Bottom
Sluggan bridge

Carrbridge was the original centre of the modern Scottish skiing industry thanks to the Austrian ski school set up by Karl Fuchs in the 1950s.

The village also hosts the World Porridge Making Championships each year with competitors fighting it out to win the Golden Spurtle. No, honestly!

Just outside the village is the popular Landmark Forest Heritage and Adventure Centre with treetop trails, a Wild Water Coaster and other adventures for all the family. The centre is open all year and includes a restaurant and snack bar.

Back on the Spey, Nethybridge is a vibrant little community and boasts the only wooden bridge across the Spey at Broomhill. Back in pre-Beeching days, travellers were thoroughly confused by the fact that a place as tiny as Nethy-

Top
Railway bridge

Top Right
**Broomhill Station aka -
Glenbogle (Strathspey
Steam Railway)**

Middle
New A9 bridge

Bottom
Broomhill bridge

bridge is served by two quite separate railway stations. Happily, the Strathspey Railway reverted to the name Broomhill station so folk know where they are. Except the station was renamed Glenbogle for the BBC television series… OK, you know the rest!

Nethybridge is host to the annual Abernethy Highland Games and Clan Grant Gathering and the games are twinned with another long-established Highland Games in the village of Turakina in New Zealand. This Abernethy is not to be confused with the town of the same name in Perthshire, which is also

Speyside Heather Centre

indirectly the likely source of the name of the famous biscuit. But the RSPB's Abernethy Forest nature reserve is here on Speyside and, as another fine remnant of the ancient Scottish pinewoods, is host to the same wonderful range of birds and mammals as the forest at Rothiemuchus, including the unique Scottish crested tit.

Nearby at Dulnain is the hugely successful Speyside Heather Centre. Over the years it has been fascinating to see a project develop from being a good idea into a thriving tourist attraction. Apart from the 300 varieties of heather, there is a garden centre, art gallery, the Clootie Dumpling restaurant, an antique centre and shop.

Walk 4 – Around Loch an Eilean

A few seconds after this photograph of Loch an Eilean was taken, a loud crack had co-author Brian Barr and everyone else scurrying for the shore. Perhaps walking on water should be left to the experts.

Start: At the visitor centre car park at the end of the metalled road.

Distance: About 5 kms

Time: Two hours (four hours for the longer version)

Grade: Easy (moderate for the longer version)

This walk could hardly be simpler. Walk round the loch and back to the visitor centre. Challenging it is not, rewarding it certainly is. Pine forests most of the way with a succession of lovely views of the castle on the island after which the loch is named. If you have a dog, keep an eye on it in case it decides to chase the deer. There are lots of picnic sites dotted around the loch and lots of other walks through the pine woods.

If you think this is too easy-peasy, you could start from the car park at the Aviemore end of Loch Morlich and follow the broad path which, after three miles or so, crosses the Cairngorm Club footbridge (also known as the Iron Bridge) and arrives at Loch an Eilean after another couple of miles. Try not to look back on the outward journey. Not that you might turn into a pillar of salt, but you will save the spectacular views of the Cairngorms for your return.

SCOTS PINE HABITAT

Between Aviemore and Cairn Gorm lies the Rothiemurchus Forest, one of the few remnants of the great Caledonian Forest in which the native Scots pine predominates. Only one per cent of the forest which covered much of the north and west of Scotland now survives. One of the main reasons for the destruction of the forest will appear in Chapter Eight, but here we briefly explore the importance of this fragile natural asset.

Scotland's pinewood forests are the essential habitat for a number of our most endangered indigenous species: wild cats, pine martens and red squirrels as well as capercaillie, the huge woodland grouse which is one of the UK's most endangered birds, and the unique Scottish crossbill.

But it's not just birds and mammals. With their open texture, Scots pines allow light to penetrate to the forest floor which becomes a rich habitat for rare plants and insects. Non-native commercial conifers, in contrast, are so densely packed that the woods are almost pitch black and the forest floor entirely sterile.

Rothiemurchus Estate is a working estate combining forestry, farming and recreation. The visitor centre at Inverdruie offers information on all the activities available on the estate including instruction on loch and river fishing. There is a shop and children's play area and the estate is open all year.

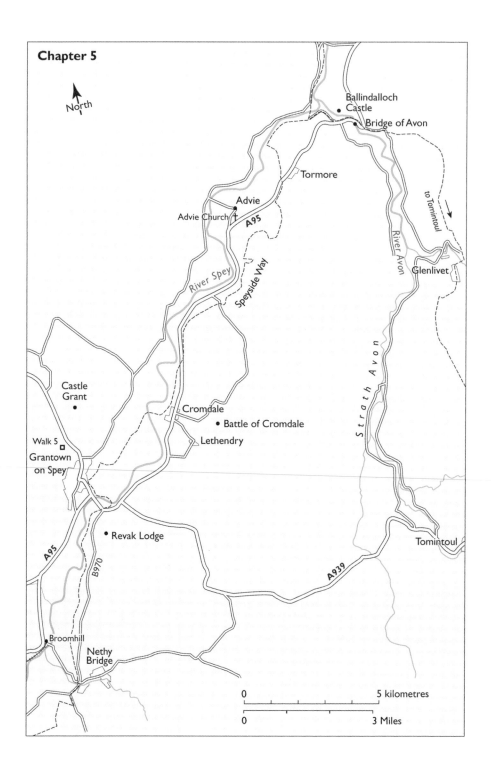

North

Ballindalloch
Castle
Bridge of Avon

Tormore

Advie

Advie Church

A95

River Spey

River Avon

to Tomintoul

Glenlivet

Speyside Way

Strath Avon

Castle
Grant

Cromdale

Battle of Cromdale

Lethendry

Walk 5

Grantown
on Spey

Revak Lodge

Tomintoul

A95

B970

A939

Broomhill

Nethy
Bridge

0   5 kilometres

0   3 Miles

Chapter Five

Battles and Boulders

Nethybridge to Ballindalloch

We are now back on the River Spey proper, and after leaving Nethybridge we come to the town of Grantown-on-Spey, the capital of Strathspey. In 1765 'Good Sir James' Grant planned a town that would attract tradesmen and their families to the area and so the old Castletown of Freuchie was transformed into a prosperous new town.

To begin with, Grantown's fortunes depended on the linen industry. By the start of the 19th century, linen was being replaced by cheap cotton from the Americas, but Grantown survived long enough to join in the Victorian tourist boom. Inevitably, the Queen herself visited, in 1860, and recorded a 'very amusing and never to be forgotten' visit, although what amused her is not recorded. Ramsay MacDonald declared 'I know no more attractive mountain resting place'.

Like so many other communities in Badenoch and Strathspey, the arrival of the railway consolidated Grantown's position as a magnet for visitors from the south. And its fortunes still substantially depend on the attractions offered

Grantown-on-Spey
Main Street

Campanile beside
Grantown Museum

to visitors: walking, fishing, cycling, white water rafting and shooting. The award-winning Grantown Museum tells the story of the town in a lively way and the Hogmanay celebrations in The Square attract revellers from a wide area.

A mile or so beyond Grantown on the A95 heading north east, you will see a sign on the right pointing to Revak Estate. It welcomes visitors with a restaurant, a shop and way-marked walks.

Castle Grant lies a mile north of Grantown and was the seat of Clan Grant – one of the oldest and most powerful clans in the Highlands. Like just about every other major clan, the Grants' history is steeped in bloodshed, treachery, mass-acres, misplaced loyalties and the occasional good deed. Again like many other clans, the Grants' fortunes were greatly affected by their choice of sides during the Jacobite risings. In the case of the Grants, however, this was complicated by the fact that various sections of the clan opted for opposing sides.

Sit up straight at the back! Here's a (potted) history lesson on the Jacobite risings.

Come back, if you will, to the 1680s, a time of intense intrigue following the death of King Charles II. Charles was succeeded by James II and VII, a Catholic. But not for long. Protestants in both England and Scotland invited his daughter Mary and her husband (and cousin) William of Orange to take the throne, and James was left feeling more and more isolated and under threat as members of his own family sided with William and Mary. James abandoned the throne and headed for France.

The trouble with having no actual monarch was that Parliament could not be summoned, but conventions were held in both England and Scotland and both voted – narrowly in Scotland – for William and Mary, although with greatly reduced powers over Parliament. In the fevered atmosphere of the time, a narrow decision by a convention was never going to settle the matter. John

Graham of Claverhouse, Viscount Dundee, stormed out of the Scottish convention with his closest followers and, along with Cameron of Locheil, set about raising an army to fight for the restoration of James (Jacobus in Latin, hence Jacobite).

On 27 July 1689, the Government army and the rebellious Highlanders met at Killiecrankie. The day ended in total victory for the Highlanders, but with the loss of their inspirational leader, 'Bonnie' Dundee. The battle also spawned the story of the Soldier's Leap when one of the Government troops escaped his pursuers by leaping the River Garry. The gap has been measured at 18ft which might be feasible with a sandpit at the other end, but with a slippery knob of rock to land on it becomes an impressive feat. Still, the imminent threat of a messy death might have put a spring in his step.

Anyway. Round two, three weeks later, was held at Dunkeld

and ended in defeat for the Jacobites, and round three brings us back to the Spey.

In May 1690 the two armies met again at the Haughs of Cromdale, two miles north east of Grantown. The Jacobites, encamped on Lethendry Hill, were waiting for the end of seed-planting so that more men could be freed to join their forces. But the Government army advan-

Cromdale Church. The bridge wasn't there in 1690

ced swiftly, and although Jacobite sentries spotted them crossing the Spey near Cromdale Church, the rapid advance caught the main Jacobite force not just unawares, but in many cases stark naked. The few who were able to resist were quickly routed and the remainder headed into the Cromdale hills where some were captured, but others managed to escape when a fog descended and made pursuit impossible. A large group were rounded up and held in Lethendry Castle.

There is a fine little walk which takes in the site of the battle. Take the road beside the hotel in Cromdale. After about a mile, follow the signs to Lethendry farm which has the remains of the castle beside it. Follow the view-point signs; the panorama is impressive with the Cairngorms to the left, Grantown and the eastern Monadhliaths ahead and the Cromdale hills behind.

Lethendry Castle, where the Jacobites were caught napping

You will see why the Government cavalry had difficulty chasing the fleeing Jacobite forces up the steep hillsides. The walk takes about an hour.

The Battle of Cromdale does not figure largely in historical texts, but it was hugely significant in the history not just of Scotland, but Britain. It marked the end of the first Jacobite uprising and by the time of the next risings – in 1715 and 1745

– enthusiasm for the Jacobite cause had waned in the Scottish Lowlands and, particularly, in England.

So, your homework is this: How would Britain be different today if the Jacobites at Cromdale had been more alert?

James Hogg, the Ettrick Shepherd, wrote a popular song about the battle. I only include the first verses a) because it goes on a bit and b) because a later bard messed about with Hogg's original and made a nonsense of the history.

As I came in by Auchindoun,
A little wee bit frae the toun,
When to the Highlands I was bound,
To view the haughs of Cromdale,
I met a man in tartan trews,
I speir'd at him what was the news;
Quo' he the Highland army rues,
That e'er we came to Cromdale.

We were in bed, sir, every man,
When the English host upon us came,
A bloody battle then began,
Upon the haughs of Cromdale.
The English horse they were so rude,
They bath'd their hooves in Highland blood,
But our brave clans, they boldly stood
Upon the haughs of Cromdale.

These days, Cromdale is a quiet little village straddling the A95 trunk road linking Aviemore with Banff on the Moray Firth. The Speyside Way, following the line of the old railway, passes close to the village.

Speyside Way near Cromdale

Five miles or so downstream from Cromdale is Advie Church which has a large Pictish symbol stone built into one of the outside walls.

On the east side of the Cromdale hills is Strath Avon where the River Avon has finally settled on its course towards the Spey, rather than the Don (see Introduction). Where the Avon is joined by the Livet lies the village of Glenlivet. This is not a book about Scotch whisky (see Chapter Six and *The Whisky River* by Robin Laing, Luath Press) but it would be odd to mention Glenlivet without mentioning its most famous product.

Glenlivet was Scotland's first legal distillery when, in 1823, the Government decided to tax and regulate the production of spirits in the Highlands and Islands. What others saw as a heinous imposition, George Smith saw as an opportunity, and, thanks to Sir Walter Scott and King George IV – yes, them again – The Glenlivet became famous. And, but for a banal accident, we would have a fine memento of the whisky's seal of royal approval.

Glenlivet Distillery

During the King's visit to Scotland (see Chapter One) Scott persuaded his distinguished visitor to sample Smith's version of the cratur[1] and slipped the empty royal glass into his back pocket. But it had been a long day and when the great writer finally crashed out – as we might say today – he also crushed the glass.

There is another Packhorse bridge over the River Livet near the village of Glenlivet, part of which managed to survive the Muckle Spate[2] of 1829.

---

[1]   'Cratur', if you're not from these parts, is an Irish/Scottish word for illicit whiskey/whisky and since Smith's whisky was entirely legal, I use the term loosely here.

[2]   It's an indication of the historic nature of the great Spey flood of 1829 that a web search of the words 'Muckle Spate' brings up references to this event alone.

And, since we are on the subject of whisky, just past Advie, on the A95, is the Tormore distillery. It was the first new distillery to be built in the 20th century, in 1958, and the architecture is striking, to say the least.

The Avon is another claimant to the title of Britain's fastest-flowing river and just before it collides with the Spey, it passes under the Bridge of Avon, built in 1754 as part of the

continued expansion of the military network following the final Jacobite uprising in 1745. Although it has been superseded by a modern structure, the old bridge has been restored and is a fine vantage point from which to view the turbulent Avon below. Overlooking the meeting of the Avon and Spey is Ballindalloch Castle, the so-called Pearl of the North, and one of very few castles in the country that has been lived in continuously by just one family – currently the MacPherson-Grants.

The original castle was built in 1546 – at least that is the date on one of its

bedroom lintels. However, foundations for an earlier building on the hill above the present castle lend credence to a story concerning the Laird of Ballindalloch.

Three times the laird attempted to build on the higher ground and three times the walls were blown down during the night. Mystified, the laird spent a night on site and heard a spectral voice saying 'Build on the coo-haugh!'

He did as he was told and the present castle on the cow pasture is the result. The castle is open to the public during the summer months.

Walk 5 – Above Grantown-on-Spey

Start: Grantown Caravan Park.

Distance: 5 kms

Time: A little over an hour

Grade: Moderate

Ask the ladies at the caravan park reception nicely and they may let you park there. Go under the railway bridge beside the waterfall to the start of the walk on the right along the old railway track. After 250m take the fairly steep path up to the left. There are two possible moments of confusion in an otherwise well-signposted route.

The first is a sign that indicates viewpoint to left and straight ahead. Not different routes to the same destination, but two different viewpoints. The one to the left can easily be taken in before heading on upwards.

Close to the top, where the path meets a forest track, there is a sign that says Viewpoint 3. Not three miles or kilometres to go, but Viewpoint No 3, which is just 100m further on.

Grantown Walk waterfall

The view is a fine panorama taking in the Cromdale Hills and the more distant Cairngorms, with an indicator board (if you need specs to read, remember to take them!)

Most of the walk is through birch, Scots pine, some willow and aspen and if you have an athletic dog you might have rabbit for supper.

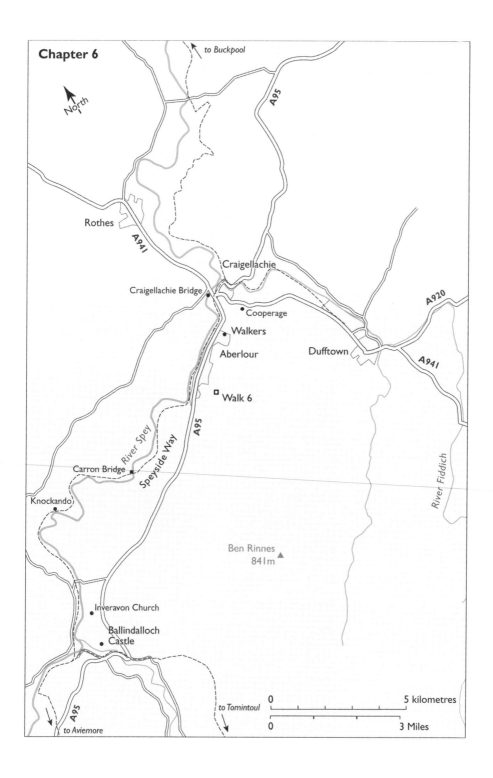

Chapter 6

North

to Buckpool

A95

Rothes

A941

Craigellachie

Craigellachie Bridge

Cooperage

Walkers

Aberlour

Dufftown

A920

A941

Walk 6

River Spey

Speyside Way

A95

Carron Bridge

River Fiddich

Knockando

Ben Rinnes
841m

Inveravon Church

Ballindalloch
Castle

to Tomintoul

0   5 kilometres

0   3 Miles

A95

to Aviemore

Chapter Six

Shortbread and Drams

Ballindalloch to Craigellachie

The Tomintoul branch of the Speyside Way joins up with the main route at Ballindalloch, and the Way continues to follow the old railway line which itself follows the twists and turns of the river. And for lovers of Scotch whisky, the names hereabouts should get the juices flowing. Glenfarclas, Cardhu, Knockando, Macallan and Aberlour are all found in just the eight miles to Craigellachie.

By now we have left the big mountains behind, the Cairngorms and the Monadhliaths, but Ben Rinnes, overlooking this section of the Spey, dominates the skyline over a large part of Moray. At 2,700ft (840m) it falls short of Munro status, but the view from the top is well worth the effort. The official story is that you can see 10 distilleries from the summit. Not so. You can see seven, but one of these is mothballed. But the way things are going, before long you may be able to see 10 windfarms. You can, however, see as far as Caithness on a clear day.

A short distance along the A95 heading towards Aberlour a sign points off to the left, marked Inveravon Church. It is well worth the detour. Four of the best-preserved Pictish symbol stones in Scotland are on the south wall of St Peter's Church. Carved about 1,500 years ago, the purpose of such stones is not certain, but they might well have accompanied a burial.

The methods used by the craftsmen show that these were regarded as important artefacts. The best preserved stone – from Moray slate – was first marked out with dotted lines and then engraved by a skilled craftsman with a mirror, an eagle and another mirror and comb. It is perhaps because of work

The Spey with Ben Rinnes in the distance

like this that the Romans named the natives Pictii, the picture or painted peoples.

Aberlour, a couple of miles before Craigellachie, is another planned village, established by another of the Grant clan. But, whereas Sir James Grant's re-naming of Castletown of Freuchie after himself stuck in the name Grantown-on-Spey, Charles Grant's attempt to have his new village named Charlestown of Aberlour has largely

Tors near the summit of Ben Rinnes

failed. Granted (so to speak!) the Ordnance Survey uses its Sunday name, but no one else does. This is Aberlour, thank you very much.

The motive for creating the new settlement was quite simply to attract workers to the distillery which the laird was also setting up, with considerable, and continuing, success it should be said. But Grant also created a rather grand and gracious village with a broad main street that would not look out of place in a much larger town. Aberlour is home to Speyside High School whose catchment area takes in the towns and villages over a wide area. And a wee story from my days as a teacher in the school leads us on to Aberlour's other claim to fame.

'Dawnald', drawled Marylou. 'Do you know Scatland?'

'Well, yes. Pretty well. Why?'

'Do you happen to know where they make Walkers shortbread?'

Marylou McBride from Texas had arrived as an exchange English teacher and she explained that she and her friends back in Texas loved the shortbread but that it was often difficult to find. She had promised not only to bring back a plentiful supply, but also – with luck – to track down the source of their favourite cookie.

'Right, Marylou. At the lunch interval, why don't you walk down to the main road, turn right and turn right again. And then you can tell me what you saw'.

Sure enough, an astonished Marylou had found Britain's largest biscuit exporter 200 yards from the school.

Pictish stones at Inveravon Church

When Joseph Walker started up his little bakery in Torphins, near Banchory on Royal Deeside in 1898 he could hardly have guessed that a century later the firm would be producing biscuits for the Prince of Wales (or the Duke of Rothesay, his title in Scotland). As well as their own range of shortbread and other cakes and biscuits, Walkers of Aberlour make Duchy Originals with organic oatmeal from the Prince's own farm.

As Joseph's fame spread, he moved to a larger shop in Aberlour and by the 1970s his grandchildren were still using his original recipes but were now exporting to over 60 countries around the world. The company now employs 1200 people, has a new factory in Elgin and recently moved its head office from the factory in Aberlour to nearby Aberlour House. The new offices were officially opened by the Duke and Duchess of Rothesay in April 2008.

Aberlour's gracious main street

What with the distillery, Walkers, the High School and the Visitors' Centre of the Speyside Way, it would be fair to say that Aberlour punches above its weight.

I have already pointed out that this is not a book about Scotch whisky, but since we are now approaching the heart of whisky country I think it would be appropriate to diverge briefly to describe the visitor facilities at the best-known distilleries but I have only chosen the ones which do not require pre-booking. Their product I leave you to evaluate for yourselves.

The **Glenlivet**, mentioned in the previous chapter, is not the most picturesque distillery, but it attracts large numbers of visitors who are offered an interesting exhibition and guided tours. It has a tearoom, and the shop has a decent selection of books and Scottish music, as well as a wide range of the distillery's own products.

Aberlour's most famous export – before Marylou's day!

Glenfiddich decided many years ago that visitor facilities would be central to their marketing policy and not just an add-on extra as in some other distilleries. In the tourist season they employ 50 guides, many of them language students on vacation. A promotional film in six languages introduces visitors to the place and its product and the tour includes the work of artists who have been com-

missioned to live and work around the distillery.

At **Glenfarclas** the distillery has a picturesque setting in the shadow of Ben Rinnes and they have a relaxed attitude towards visitors. Tours take place when there are enough people to form a group and the reception room has wall panelling and memorabilia from the P&O liner *Empress of Australia*. I did ask, but I still don't know why!

The little back road, the B9102, that connects Grantown with Craigellachie – well worth a diversion if you're not in a

Glenfarclas Distillery
with ornamental still

Prince Charles inspects
production of Duchy
Originals

hurry – takes you past the **Cardhu** distillery. The story goes that – as elsewhere – most of the crofters in the area had their (illicit) stills. Helen Cumming's house was the first the excisemen came upon on their way from Elgin. With a few minutes' warning she could hide the still and get a big baking going. The baking smells masked the smell of distilling. The visitors never noticed the red flag on her pole warning the others that the guagers were around. As the pressure on the illegal operations increased, the locals decided that one of them should become legal and that was Helen at Cardhu. Hers became the second official distillery after Glenlivet.

Like many other distilleries, the buildings at **Glen Grant** are unlikely to win any architectural awards, but then these are industrial production units, whatever romantic mystique may be conjured up by the marketing departments. But its new Italian owners apparently have plans to improve the visitor experience. As it is, one highlight is the post-tour dram in a replica of the founder's sitting room. It would be fair to say his taste was eclectic! The other unique feature of the site is the gracious Victorian gardens set in mature woodland.

The gardens at
Glen Grant

But if it's a photograph you want, **Strathisla** distillery is the place. I wish I could claim the credit for the one here (see Acknowledgements). It is a very pretty building with a working (by electricity) millwheel and some of the buildings date back to 1786, supporting the company's claim to have the oldest working distillery in the Highlands. The River Isla flows past the back of the distillery and sea trout can often be seen attempting to jump the waterfall. I have also seen an otter, cormorants and a kingfisher on this stretch of the river – and No, I hadn't been over-indulging at the time!

The only distillery in the ruined cathedral city (it's the cathedral that's ruined, not the city) of Elgin is **Glen Moray** and they have only fairly recently started taking the visitor business seriously. Your tour guide might well be a production worker temporarily withdrawn from front-line duties, and the visitor centre offers light snacks as well as samples of the whisky. Indeed, by pre-booking and paying, you can have the distillery manager as guide and some well-informed tasting as well.

Deep and crisp
and steaming.
Strathisla Distillery

Dalwhinnie Distillery

Knockando Wool Mill

THE SPEY: FROM SOURCE TO SEA

Aberlour distillery welcomes visitors but strongly advises booking in advance. There are two tours (or should that be "performances"?) per day and they last two hours. Although the visit is not cheap, in includes a whisky tasting and the chance to buy a personally-labelled bottle of the product.

And then there's **Dalwhinnie** distillery, which isn't strictly a Speyside whisky, but

since it is on the River Truim which is a tributary of the Spey, I'll allow it. And it is the first distillery visitors coming north on the A9 come across as they make the long descent from Drumochter Pass. The setting may be a little bleak, but the distillery is bonnie, with a good shop, and it draws the crowds in the summer months.

Knockando also has a distillery but it does not have visitor facilities. The village does, however, have another claim to fame. Knockando Wool Mill may not look like much, but this is a Category A listed building, perhaps not for its architectural merit – though it certainly has character! – but rather for what it is, what it contains, and the history behind it.

It is a local working wool mill containing all the old machinery to turn fleece into tweed. Most mills like this died a natural death either side of World War II. But Hugh Jones, living in London in 1970, faced an intriguing choice. He could either do the sensible thing and become a teacher. Or he could, without any experience or background knowledge apart from a love of old machinery, answer the advert he'd seen and buy and run a wee old wool mill deep in the woods of distant Speyside. The wool won, of course, or I wouldn't be telling you the story.

Thirty years and countless garments later, it began to dawn on Hugh that, as a one-man operation working a piece of priceless history, the expertise and the mill itself would be lost forever when he retired. So a trust was set up, not just to preserve the working mill, but to develop the project in other ways.

The existence of the mill came to national notice when in 2004 Knockando Wool Mill won the Scottish section of the BBC's *Restoration* competition, presented by Griff Rhys Jones and offering £2.5 million of Heritage Lottery money to the winner. Knockando didn't win the UK final, but the know-how and publicity they gathered in the process was put to good use. They applied for grants from the lottery, from Europe and from Historic

Carron Bridge

Scotland and they've raised the best part of the money they would have won. So the funding is in place to realise the trust's ambitious plans for the mill.

Of all the facets of the projects, the two that most appeal to me are the workshop in which textile students will be able to hone their skills, and the restored waterwheel, not to provide power for the machinery, but to provide heat for the buildings.

The section of the Speyside Way between Ballindalloch and Craigellachie is 12 miles long and follows the line of the old Strathspey railway, which means walkers have two memorable structures to negotiate. The listed Carron Bridge is unique in that the single bridge carried both road and rail traffic. This photograph of the bridge was chosen by singer Annie Lennox as her contribution to the Sight Savers International charity campaign, not only for the beauty of the surroundings but because her gamekeeper grandfather used to fish the Spey at this point.

Walkers on the Way also get the chance to test the echo in the 100m tunnel between Craigellachie and Aberlour and, because the builders of the railway followed the course of the river, this whole section of the Way is one of the best methods of absorbing the 'feel' of this middle section of the Spey. Aberlour also has the Victoria – or 'Penny' – footbridge connecting the village with Wester Elchies on the far bank.

Craigellachie Bridge

THE SPEY: FROM SOURCE TO SEA

Just before the village of Craigellachie is the bridge of the same name. Built by Thomas Telford in 1814, it is now an A listed building and open only to cyclists and pedestrians. There is no question about the elegance of the bridge, but there is another story about it which I have not been able to confirm.

Telford liked to discuss his projects in advance with local people, and when he showed his plans for Craigellachie Bridge to the locals, they praised

The old Speyside Railway tunnel, now the Speyside Way, and a chance to test the echo

Mallorca? Tenerife? No, it's the Costa Craig!

Craigellachie Hotel

the design but thought it was not high enough to withstand a serious flood of the river. Telford added 5ft to the original height and when the Muckle Spate arrived in 1829, his was the only bridge over the entire length of the Spey to survive. True? I don't know. Should be true? Definitely!

Just below the bridge is a feature known (by me, at least!) as Costa Craig, a shingle beach on the river much favoured by local youngsters on a sunny summer day. Good thing my parents aren't around to tell them how dangerous it is!

Craigellachie boasts not one, but two distilleries in the vicinity, as befits the settlement at the junction of two of the rivers most closely associated with whisky – the Spey and the Fiddich.

The Craigellachie distillery is another modern building and it has no visitor centre. And the Macallan is on the other side of the Spey. Another whisky-related feature is just outside the village on the Dufftown road – the Speyside Cooperage with a visitor centre explaining how 100,000 second hand barrels a year are reconstructed and give the malt whisky stored in them some of the flavour of their previous occupants – sherry, port, Madeira etc.

The main hotel in the village, the Craigellachie Hotel, is not quite as substantial as it appears. It looks at first glance like a typical grand Victorian lodge but it is made of wood, rendered on the outside to look like stone. There is also the Highlander Inn in the village and the Fiddichside Inn just after the bridge

Speyside Cooperage

over the River Fiddich. The village also has two art galleries, although sadly the village shop has been turned into a hairdressing salon.

Walk 6 – Linn Falls

Start: Leave the Speyside Way at Lour Burn and a path opposite the Aberlour Distillery

Distance: 5 kms

Time: At least an hour

Grade: Easy, but can be muddy after rain

Calling a waterfall the Linn Falls is a bit like calling a hill Binn Hill. I think it's called tautology in polite circles. 'Binn' means hill. 'Linn' means waterfall.

The Falls are approached by leaving the Speyside Way at Lour Burn, passing the old packhorse bridge and crossing the busy main road to a path opposite the Aberlour Distillery.

The falls seem to have had particular significance for the ancient Celts here- abouts and Druids are said to have worshipped there. It is a beautiful setting but there is something slightly spooky about the place. They say local people are afraid of being lured to a watery grave, but I don't believe a word of it. Aaaaarghhh! Kersplash!

It's about 5 kms round trip, allow at least an hour.

Linn Falls

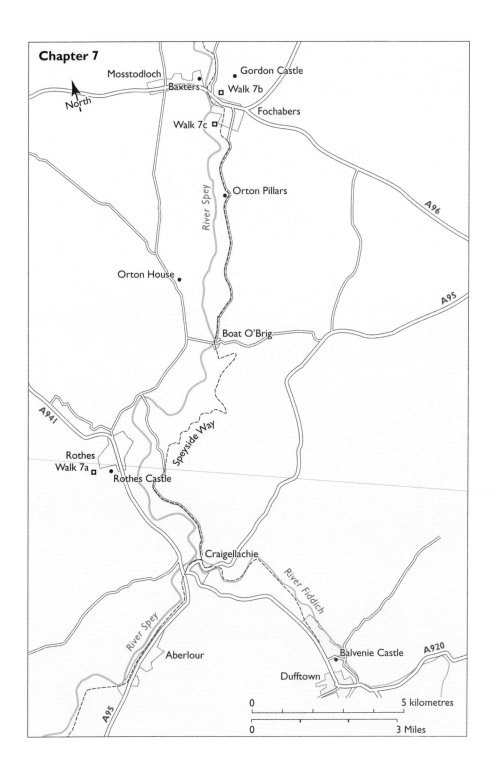

Chapter 7

Mosstodloch

Gordon Castle

Baxters

Walk 7b

North

Fochabers

Walk 7c

River Spey

Orton Pillars

A96

Orton House

A95

Boat O'Brig

A941

Speyside Way

Rothes
Walk 7a
Rothes Castle

Craigellachie

River Fiddich

River Spey

Balvenie Castle

A920

Aberlour

Dufftown

A95

0   5 kilometres

0   3 Miles

Chapter Seven

Soup, Salmon and Fiddles

Craigellachie to Fochabers

We are now in Moray. Actually, we've been in Moray since Ballindalloch, but the surroundings now are distinctively different from Badenoch and Strathspey. Not just the distilleries all around, but the landscape and even the sports grounds are quite different. We are also now into Highland League football rather than shinty country. Ask hereabouts what a caman is, and folk might guess one of these wee crocodile things! But before heading further downstream, I want to take a small detour to Dufftown. After all, the Speyside Way does exactly the same thing, offering a spur from Craigellachie to Dufftown.

We've already come across Dufftown in the context of James MacPherson, the fiddle and the clock tower. But the town's real claim to fame is that it is The Whisky Capital of the World. To be honest, it's hard to argue with the claim. It produces more malt whisky than any other town in Scotland, and Dufftown claims to generate more export revenue *per capita* than anywhere else in Britain.

It's another of those towns and villages that have changed names a few times. First it was Laichie. Then the Earl of Fife decided to start a new town

**The Spey
at Orton**

Balvenie Castle

called Balvenie, after the nearby Balvenie Castle, and then re-named it Dufftown. And the castle, now a ruin, has had some distinguished visitors in its seven centuries or so. Edward I of England called by, as did Mary Queen of Scots. In 1689, following their victory at Killiecrankie, the Jacobite forces occupied the castle, only to be expelled by Government troops following Culloden. It also has strong links with the Earls of Comyn.

The Speyside Whisky Festival is held in the town over four or five days every autumn with a truly staggering range of tastings, talks, tours and ceilidhs. There is also the whisky museum, a whisky shop with an awe-inspiring range of bottles and a historic (but not very) railway that runs between Dufftown and Keith during summer weekends.

Back to the Spey, however, and the town of Rothes. And if there's a town that might contest Dufftown's mighty claims, it's Rothes. No less than five distilleries, including the famous Glen Grant, as well as a large animal feed plant using the by-products of many Speyside distilleries.

It may be a modest whisky town now, but Rothes has had its moments in the limelight of Scottish history, although the only tangible reminder is one wall of a once formidable castle. Edward I used Rothes Castle as a base for his punitive campaign against the Scots that culminated in the theft of the Stone of Destiny from Scone Palace. But back in the 17th century, the good law-abiding folk of

Rothes had what remained of the castle removed (apart from the one wall) because it had become a haven for 'thieves and vagabonds'.

Heading on north east from Rothes, we pass into the lands belonging to Orton Estate. While there are stretches of the Spey beside sizeable communities, such as Grantown, Aberlour and Rothes, where fishing is owned and run by local associations and therefore cheap or free to locals, most of the banks are the preserve of the private estates – as is the shooting. For keen anglers with a penny or two in their pockets some names are mouth-watering: Castle Grant, Tulchan, Ballindalloch, Wester Elchies, Delfur, Gordon Castle.

In the course of photographing the remarkable Orton earth pillars I became more and more intrigued by the buzz about the estate. It is not big compared with some; about three miles of river positioned between it and the B9015 Rothes to Mosstodloch road, a strip about a mile wide with rough woodland close to the Spey and mixed farmland with copses up to the main road. The copses were important because the place was hoaching with young pheasants.

What had been old farmhouses and cottages have been converted into fishing lodges and holiday lets. Orton House, which I remembered from way back as down-at-heel and uninhabited, has been restored to its Georgian splendour. A couple of tractors in the fields; anglers and ghillies; visitors, some of

All that remains of
Rothes Castle

whom were obviously regulars, of different nationalities. A dozen cars were parked discreetly by the Estate Office. There was obviously a guiding force behind this operation – someone with the finance to back the vision.

As a callow youth, Peter Millar received some firm advice from his father: 'There isn't room for both of us being in charge here at Orton. Go out there and earn your living.' Which he did, as a chartered accountant, working in Glasgow, Dundee, Wall Street and Abu Dhabi before he made his way back to Orton. Half the cars parked outside the Estate Office belonged to employees of his investment company which shared the converted barn.

Meeting Peter Millar was a pleasure and his glimpses into the history of the Wharton-Duff family were interesting. He estimated the estate's annual contribution to the local economy at around £500,000 which, multiplied many times over the length of the river, means that these estates are major financial contributors to the coffers of Highland and Moray Councils.

The onset of mechanisation and the downturn in farming income means

Fishing where the Avon
meets the Spey

THE SPEY: FROM SOURCE TO SEA

that, to survive, they have had to diversify and become, in effect, sophisticated businesses. In the case of large estates like Glenlivet and Rothiemurchus, a by-product has been a huge range of activities encouraging public access and tourism. Freedom-to-roam legislation has largely put an end to the old 'Trespassers will be prosecuted' signs – though there are obviously tensions during the shooting seasons.

Fishing at Orton earth pillars. Watch out for the whirlpool!

That said, private ownership of huge tracts of Scottish land, particularly in the Highlands and Borders, empowers the owner for either good or ill. The management of the land within the Spey catchment area is generally benign but there are a few exceptions. And even the good can be a mixed blessing if one is dependent on the landlord's goodwill.

Brigs at Boat O'Brig

As to the fishing, the news is that from a fairly desperate low towards the end of last century, Spey salmon catches are now very healthy – at least in part due to the anglers' self-imposed policy of returning most caught fish to the river.

I asked the ghillie who was supervising the angler in the

Caught, but about to be returned

photograph how the day had gone. 'Good', he said cautiously, 'but not a Klondyke'. I tried to imagine an angling Klondyke and got as far as four quarter pound trout in a frying pan by a wee loch, but I'm not sure he would have been very impressed.

Boat O'Brig, just beyond Orton, started life as Brig O'Boat when a bridge replaced a ferry across the river. The bridge was swept away and it became Boat O'Brig. The bridge was rebuilt but Brig O'Boat O'Brig seemed a bit of a mouthful so they left it at Boat O'Brig. Actually there are two bridges, one carrying the Aberdeen to Inverness railway and the other the B9103 from Mulben to Orton.

There is no better way of completing this section of the river than by following the Speyside Way giving splendid views of the valley of the mature Spey. And there's a surprise in store in the form of the Orton earth pillars, a weird jumble of red clay cliffs overlooking the river at Ordiquish. It's possible to get to the pillars by car, taking the small road opposite the museum in Fochabers and following it for a mile to a car park close to the pillars.

I met a ghillie a few years back who told me he'd spent the whole day fishing from a boat on the Spey. I asked how he'd anchored the boat, since a day of rowing against the flow would be unthinkable. 'No, no,' he said, 'I didn't anchor. I just went into the whirlpool at the Orton pillars and went roon' an' roon''. I tried to take a photograph from beside the pillars one day, but the ground was steep and crumbly and I was afraid I'd go doon and doon, an roon' an' roon', and droon and droon. Sorry about that. It works better spoken than written!

Gordon Castle

And then we reach Fochabers. The original village lay to the north, nearer Gordon Castle, but the fourth Duke of Gordon felt it was all getting a bit crowded out there and in 1776 had plans drawn up for a new village on the present site. The Duke and his Duchess led turbulent personal lives and the family may have left enormous debts, but from the staff of Gordon Castle there emerged individuals and families who were to leave substantial legacies to the local and wider community.

Take Alexander Milne, for example. Born in 1742, Milne got a job as a footman at the castle, but he was ordered to cut off his long red hair to make room for the powdered wig required by the job. He refused, and found another position as batman to an army officer who was about to leave for the New World. They wound up in New Orleans and Milne set about making his fortune, first in the hardware business and then in brick-making. His success was assured by the great fire of 1788 and Milne used the profits to buy up large tracts of land alongside Lake Pontchartrain, an area of the city still called Milneburg.

Milne was greatly influenced by the frustration he'd felt as a young man having to kowtow to the duke and determined to do what he could to give youngsters – especially young black men – the education that would improve their prospects. The Colored Waif's Home he endowed helped the young Louis Armstrong to become the world's greatest jazz trumpeter. The home was re-named the Milne Boys' Home in the 1930s and ceased to be a childrens' home in the 1980s. The building, already somewhat neglected, was badly damaged by Hurricane Katrina.

But Milne had not forgotten Fochabers. His will also endowed a school which he hoped would mean young people in his home town would not be forced into working for the estate. The original Milne's High School, at the top end of the village, became increasingly cramped as a secondary school, so a new senior school was built. The original building might have languished, but the Moray Council, despite being strapped for cash, had the vision to renovate the old building and turn it into the primary school. It is a handsome building by day and spectacular when it is floodlit at night.

Chapel at Milne Boys'
Home, New Orleans

Marylou McBride from Texas (see Chapter Six), amazed that the world-famous Walkers shortbread came from the village of Aberlour, would have been equally impressed that the world-famous Baxters products emerge from a factory beside the Spey between Fochabers and the village of Mosstodloch. Baxters employs up to 1,000 workers and, like Walkers, re-

Milne's School

Baxters Highland Village

mains a family-owned business. The visitors' centre, Baxters Highland Village, attracts getting on for a quarter of a million visitors a year and there are factory tours, a museum and audio-visual presentations. And, of course, shops.

The story of Baxters is remarkably similar to that of Walkers of Aberlour (see Pp 74–75). George Baxter started the firm in 1868, just 30 years before Joseph Walker began making his shortbread. George's wife Margaret made jams and jellies in the back of their grocers shop in Fochabers and when they gained the approval of the Duke of Gordon, their popularity spread.

In 1914, George's son William and his wife Ethel bought a plot of land from the Duke, built a small factory, and Ethel developed a range of soups, including the iconic Royal Game Soup. And now, like Walkers, Baxters export their products all around the world. And guess who turned up to help the Baxters celebrate 125 years of production in Fochabers? Prince Charles, of course.

Fochabers Canal under construction in 1905, and today

Another accomplished son of Fochabers is William Marshall. Anyone with a passing interest in Scottish fiddle music has heard of Scott Skinner and Neil Gow. Not so many have heard of William Marshall, although he was arguably as fine a composer as the other two. According to Robert Burns, he was the Strathspey King of his day such was his skill with the traditional dance form. So why isn't he better known? I'll tell you why from harsh personal experience.

I have a diploma that testifies that I can make respectable sounds on the violin. I have even been asked to judge other people playing the fiddle. One lunchtime, as a music teacher at Buckie High School, I decided to spend the break practising Marshall's Strathspey *Craigellachie Brig*. In walked James Alexander, then and still a renowned fiddle teacher and performer. I was struggling and quietly cursing Marshall. I asked for help. James smiled quietly and then produced a source-book in which the great man strongly advised amateur

Fochabers High Street in 1965, and as it is today

players against attempting his tunes. Thanks for telling me!

The same James Alexander, following a visit to a Celtic festival on the Isle of Man, was inspired to establish Speyfest in Fochabers in 1993 which, with community support, continues to be a major event on the Scottish folk-festival calendar, bringing performers from the British Isles and abroad.

The Christie family have also made their mark on Fochabers. The family's nursery business was started in 1820 and by the 1960s it had become one of the country's biggest suppliers of forest seedlings. The garden centre in the village now employs 25 people and the family also own shops and a caravan park. In 1982, the late George Christie and his wife bought a disused church and established the Fochabers Museum which has a remarkable and eclectic collection of antiques and memorabilia.

And a final claim to fame for Fochabers. It was one of the first villages of its size in the north of Scotland to be entirely powered by electricity, thanks to a unique hydro-electric scheme. Around 1905, the Duke of Richmond and Gordon fancied having Gordon Castle lit by electric light, so he built a canal to provide the water and a small power station, and anyone in Fochabers who wanted could join the grid. The remnants of the canal, although somewhat overgrown, can still be seen.

You'll see, then, that Fochabers, population 1,800, is a lively place with a strong community spirit. But Fochabers has a problem. Here is a well-planned village with a picturesque square, fine churches and an interesting selection of shops. But its main street, designed for the horse and cart, is the A96 linking Aberdeen and Inverness, one of the busiest roads in Scotland. The story of Fochabers' attempt to acquire a by-pass would make an interesting – but depressing – book in itself. Perhaps by the time this book is on its fourth reprint the by-pass will have happened. Perhaps pigs will have become pilots!

Walk 7 – Around Rothes and Fochabers

a   Walk up the hill from the middle of Rothes via the castle wall (watch out for 'thieves and vagabonds'). Pass the golf clubhouse (if you have a car you can ask nicely and they'll let you park here) and follow the forestry track. Turn right towards the waterfall (signposted) and on down to the riverside. Resist following through to the distillery and look for a small track created by mountain bikers on the right. Climb steadily and you are back where you started. A pech up at the end, but otherwise gentle. Allow an hour.

b   Beside the Gordon Chapel in Castle Street there is a mysterious-looking green door set into the high wall. Push it open (it's OK, it's not as private as it looks) and it leads to a lovely 20-minute walk round the loch (it's called The Lake for some reason on OS maps), rich in bird life – ducks, coots, moorhens and a resident pair of nesting mute swans.

c   As the A96 heading west curves out of Fochabers towards Baxters, there is a sign opposite the cricket pitch pointing to 'Community Woodland Walks'. After 200m there is a car park at the memorial gardens. Cross the burn, notice some minor civil engineering works to allow sea trout up the burn, and pass a few houses, after which the tarred road becomes a forest track. On the right are the overgrown remains of the hydro-electric canal. The route is circular, out alongside the river and back through the woods. The going is flat, but can be muddy. It is a favourite dog-walk for locals so wildlife has mostly been scared off or eaten, but I have seen red squirrels, roe deer and (heard rather than seen) woodpeckers. The long-necked diver sort of birds flying up and down the river are mergansers or goosanders on the school run.

Allow an hour.

Birdlife on The Lake, Fochabers

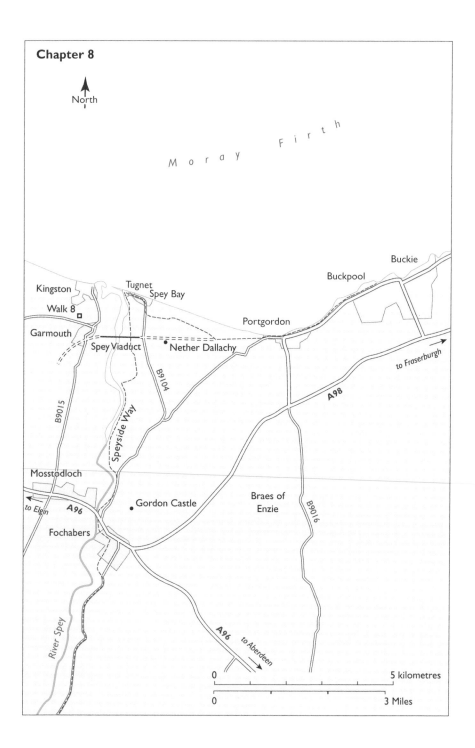

North

Moray Firth

Kingston

Tugnet
Spey Bay

Buckie

Buckpool

Walk 8

Portgordon

Garmouth

Spey Viaduct

Nether Dallachy

to Fraserburgh

B9104

A98

B9015

Speyside Way

Mosstodloch

Braes of
Enzie

B9016

to Elgin

A96

Gordon Castle

Fochabers

River Spey

A96

to Aberdeen

0   5 kilometres

0   3 Miles

Chapter Eight

Ships, Picts and the Sea

Fochabers to Spey Bay

Any book about the Spey must, at some point, tackle (sorry!) the matter of fishing, particularly salmon fishing. We touched on the subject earlier with hooks in thumb and the Orton Estate, but I had better establish my own credentials, if you'll pardon the expression.

You already know that my brother Brian and I fished burns and wee lochs for trout and we sometimes even caught them, rather than each other. But I'll have you know that I've had bigger fish than trout on the end of my line. In the early '50s proper fishing rods were in short supply and dauntingly expensive. But some bright entrepreneur realised that tank radio aerials from redundant hardware after World War II could be turned into rudimentary rods. We were given one each for Christmas.

Fishing just below the Falls of Truim (see map for Chapter Two) I was almost yanked off my 11-year-old feet. Whatever it was, it was bigger and stronger than me. It could only be one thing. As I yelled for help, I knew I was battling a seal. I had nothing as fancy as a reel but my line was very strong so,

Falls of Truim – scene of an epic battle between boy and beast. Beast won.

faced with the monster and a deep pool directly ahead, I opted for survival and abandoned the rod.

I know, I know. It wasn't a seal. You don't find many seals in the upper reaches of Highland rivers. It was a salmon, and a mighty big one at that. It just seemed a shame that a piece of equipment that might well have survived the North Africa campaign ended up being drowned by a salmon. And a salmon, on the last exhausting leg of its journey to the spawning grounds, had to get there with a tank aerial in tow.

An expert in these things told me that the art of Spey casting can be learned in a morning. Aye, maybe. I remembered years ago my long-suffering tutor was Donald MacKenzie from Lewis (and from long experience of adjudicating at the National Mod I can say that no-one is better equipped in the art of casting a line to get a satisfactory result than a Lewisman). Anyway, I got my line in so many fankles that Donald, in amongst what I took to be friendly words in Gaelic (but might not have been), suggested in English that I might care to admire the scenery while he looked after the catching of the fish. Which he duly did. So there you have my credentials as a salmon angler. (See also, Appendix Two.)

As we leave Fochabers, we are just five miles from Spey Bay and the sea. The Speyside Way follows the right (east) bank of the river through woods to

Garmouth

start with and then on to open ground and then passes beside the Spey Viaduct which carried the old coastal railway. It's worth a brief detour to stand under the viaduct and you can appreciate the power and speed of the river, especially if it is in spate. This is also a good spot to see the signs of the river's uncertainty about which is the best way to reach the sea and why this is the only major river in Scotland not to have a city at its mouth.

Over on the west bank are the villages of Garmouth and Kingston. Take a look at the architecture at Garmouth and you will notice that it is markedly different from the norm in north east Scotland. My own view is that Scottish rural architecture is more interesting than that of Ireland which leapt from turf-roofed

hovels to haciendas and bungalows with little in between, thanks, in part, to the laws of land inheritance and, more recently, grants from the European Community. On the other hand, Scottish farms and village houses are generally much less interesting than their counterparts in England.

The typical Scottish farmhouse was built between 100 and 150 years ago when the laws of inheritance and land reform created larger farms. It is stone built, has some character and blends into the countryside. But it is short on the antiquity and architectural variety of houses in rural England. And they are much smaller than their continental counterparts. The ground floor of my own cottage, built around 1900 as a 40-acre farm, would comfortably fit into the extended kitchen of French relations whose Jura farmhouse was built 100 years earlier with a similar acreage. And many Scottish village houses were generally part of an overall plan with straight lines and 90 degree angles, built alongside or at right angles to a road.

Garmouth, on the contrary, emerged haphazardly from the Middle Ages, has a meandering main street, a mixture of architectural styles reflecting the ages, and a handsome hostelry that is amongst its older buildings. The village is also the site of the annual Maggie Fair which dates back to 1587.

Garmouth was also the site of one of the greatest non-events in Scottish history. In 1650, Charles II arrived by sea, seeking restoration to the throne

and, with his fingers crossed, so to speak, signed the Solemn League and Covenant promising that, in return for Scottish support, he would, after his coronation, make the entire kingdom Presbyterian. There is a plaque to commemorate the event. Or non-event. Because Charles blithely reneged on his promise.

It is one of the oddities of the teaching of Scottish history in my day that we never heard of the Battle of Cromdale (see Chapter Five) whose outcome had a profound impact on the future of Scot-

land, whereas the Solemn League and Covenant was a favourite exam question. Discuss. The fact is, there was never any possibility that Charles, if
restored, could impose Presbyterianism on England. Call him a pragmatist, or
call him a liar. And anyway, despite my own Presbyterian background, given the
flowering of the arts after the Restoration, this was no bad thing.

If you require further proof of the Spey's unpredictable meanderings, then
the history of Garmouth provides it. It was once a thriving port exporting much
local produce to Europe, including manganese ore from a mine between
Tomintoul and the Lecht whose remains can still be seen. But the river moved
away, the sea retreated and Garmouth was left stranded. So Kingston started up
as the port for Garmouth. But then Kingston itself suddenly acquired national,
even international, prominence as the unlikely site of one of Britain's most
important shipbuilding centres.

In 1783 Ralph Dodsworth and William Osborne, timber merchants from
Hull, had a bright idea. Here was a big forest at Glenmore, east of Aviemore.
Here was a big river flowing to the sea. So they bought most of the forest from
the Duke of Gordon and set about felling the trees, squaring them off and float-
ing them down the Spey in rafts.

Meanwhile, down at the mouth of the Spey, they added a storey to Red Corff
House (now called Dunfermline House) whose origins go back to 1654 when
stone from the ruined Urquhart Priory – an offshoot of Dunfermline Abbey –
was used as building material. They built a canal and slipway beside the house,
and two sawmills, one powered by wind, the other by water.

The two entrepreneurs didn't hang around. The first ship was completed
in 1785, and by 1791, 19 had been completed by what was now called the
Glenmore Company. A village had grown up to house the workers and the two
men named it Kingston after their home town Kingston-upon-Hull.

According to Jim Skelton, in his account of shipbuilding at Kingston,
Speybuilt, over 500 ships were built between 1785 and 1890, most of them
schooners and barques. And all without a harbour or even a breakwater. And
all gone, apart from a few of the original houses. Gone also the Spey Floaters,
the men who deftly guided the rafts of timber the 50 miles from near Aviemore
to Kingston negotiating sharp bends, sunken rocks, rapids and even the occasional drought.

By the way, if the intricacies of Spey casting do not float your boat, try
spinning something bright and shiny off the shore on an incoming tide at
Kingston. Sea trout and sea bass are the thing here. The best test of the conditions is this: if there are locals fishing, it's worth a try. If not, it's not. And don't
worry that you are competing with them. It's a big pool, the Moray Firth, and
if the fish are on a coastal run, there's plenty to go round.

On the East side of the river, opposite Garmouth and Kingston, is Nether Dallachy and there you will find an intriguing nameplate on a cottage which leads me to the Battle of Mons Graupius and a theory I have about its location. But first, we have to go back to Roman Britain around 83 or 84 AD…

Historians are pretty well agreed that the result of the Battle of Mons Graupius was a victory for the Roman army led by Agricola over the last of the northern British tribes, the Caledonii. Historians pretty much disagree on where the battle took place. Some think it happened near the hill of Bennachie in Aberdeenshire, others that it took place near Perth, others still suggest Sutherland. The only written 'evidence' is the account of the battle by Tacitus, written in 98 AD. My theory goes like this…

Fact 1: The name on the gable end of this cottage near Nether Dallachy is, as you can see, Roman Camp Cottage, and there is, indeed, evidence of a small Roman camp having been established here.

Fact 2: The camp here is far too small to have been a marching camp for the 20,000 men of Agricola's main army which had been sent north to complete the subjugation of the troublesome tribes. But the Roman fleet had been sent ahead of the main force to impress the locals and set up a supply base. The Nether Dallachy camp fits with the Roman navy rounding Buchan Ness and put-

An intriguing name

ting into the coast to await the arrival of the army. Admittedly, the site is now a mile or so from the sea, but – given the constantly-changing nature of the coastline – might well have been much closer 2,000 years ago.

Fact 3: There is a much larger Roman camp at Grange, a couple of miles east of Keith, certainly large enough to have been a marching camp for the whole force and it appears to be the most northerly point of the Roman expedition.

Puzzle 1: Here is this huge force, poised to march over the Braes of Enzie and down into the fertile land of the Moray Coast and a reunion with their navy and their supplies. But they stopped. Why?

Evidence 1: Tacitus, son-in-law of Agricola and embedded war correspondent, describes the battle taking place beneath a nearby hill. The Balloch overlooks the Grange site. The Latin for hill is *mons*, which became *mont, monte* or *mount* in later European languages. The old Celtic name for a hump was

Pass of the Grange. Site of the battle?

A significant name?

graup, or *graupius* in the Latin version. The farm closest to the site at Grange is Mont Grew, locally pronounced Grau.

Evidence 2: Spin doctors may be older than we imagine. Perhaps Agricola stopped because the opposition – 30,000 determined locals – was much stronger than he expected. He might have won the battle, but the majority of the defeated Caledonii melted away into the dense woodland, perhaps to fight another day. So maybe the conversation between Agricola and his son-in-law went something like this:

'OK, Tacitus old chap, you report back that we've won a famous victory, job done. Now let's forget this Godforsaken place and get back to defending more important parts of the Empire. Make it sound good. Give the tabloids (or perhaps he said 'tablets') a lively story.'

Which is exactly what Tacitus did. His colourful description of the battle includes hearing the Celtic leader, Calgacus, proclaiming to his troops: 'They rob, kill and rape and this they call Roman rule. They make a desert, and call it *Pax Romana*'. Historians take the quote with a large pinch of salt. How could Tacitus have understood what a Celtic leader was saying? It may, indeed, have been an elaboration by the war correspondent, but it is not impossible. The Roman army included auxiliaries from other parts of the Empire, and amongst them might have been some from other conquered northern tribes from Gaul and southern Britain. The Gauls certainly would have spoken the same language (see Chapter One) as Calgacus and his Celts. Translation would not have been a problem.

Conclusion: The Battle of Mons Graupius took place at Grange, Banffshire. So there.

Be that as it may, you are now approaching Spey Bay and you are on the edge of an amazing ecological feature. This is a living, changing flood plain that is based on shingle, but with grasses, flowers, reed beds and all the bird life that goes with them. The car park at Kingston gives a flavour of the place, but the walk below gives the full experience.

But before we reach the end of our journey, walkers following the Speyside Way are not quite finished yet. The Way turns right at the sea and you have a pleasant five miles along the Moray coast to the official start/end of the Way at Buckpool harbour. To be frank, it may turn out to be a bit of an anti-climax. A couple of stone slabs mark the end. No tearoom. Not even any boats. But do not despair. A little further onwards and upwards and you are in Buckie and an entirely different Scotland, in the world of the north east fishing communities.

The fishing ports are not what they once were, of course, but Buckie still has a busy harbour with the remnants of a great fishing fleet and shipbuilding and repairing, and the Fishing Heritage Museum. Buckie is also the start/end of another fine walk – the Moray Coastal Trail which leads through Portessie,

Keep right on to the end of the Way...

Findochty, pronounced 'Finechty'

Bow Fiddle Rock

Marshall mosaic with ice house behind

Findochty, Portknockie, Cullen, Sandend, Portsoy and on eastwards. This is also the route of the annual Six Harbour Walk. Look out for the amazing pet cemetery at Cullen and the spectacular Bow Fiddle Rock just beyond Portknockie which is shaped like… Oh, never mind.

We, however, end our journey at Spey Bay. And there is no anti-climax here. The great river surges out into the surf and there is much to see and enjoy, even if there is no great city and port. There is the Tugnet Ice House, in its day by far the largest in the country and the centrepiece of a huge salmon fishing station. The ice house was built in 1830, but salmon fishing on an industrial scale dates back to the middle of the 18th century. The process was simple. Blocks of river ice were stored in the thick-walled building and used throughout the year to preserve the salmon before their long journey to market. Some of the other buildings have been converted

The journey begins. Burn leaving Loch Spey

Journey's end. Spey Bay nature reserve

into the Moray Firth Wildlife Centre and the mosaics nearby were designed and built by local schoolchildren and include a portrait of William Marshall (see Chapter Seven).

The area is designated the Spey Bay Nature Reserve and is a favourite fishing spot for osprey. With any luck you should also be able to spot dolphins out in the Firth chasing the salmon and sea trout.

So, we have come from Loch Spey, with its typical small hill loch trout, to Spey Bay and its salmon and dolphins. Note how the river reaches the sea as wild as when it started. And take a moment to think back on the huge and spectacular catchment area of mountains and lochs, the rivers and burns, that drain into this dark, peaty waterway thundering into the Moray Firth.

This has been the Spey: from Source to Sea.

Water tower near Garmouth

Walk 8 – Kingston

Now listen, if you've just finished the Speyside Way, we'll let you off. But if you've arrived at Kingston by car, no excuses are permitted.

Start: At the car park in Kingston

Distance: 3 kms

Time: About an hour

Grade: Easy

Head along Lein Road and have a second look at the house on the corner; set squares, plumb lines and spirit levels clearly had no part in its construction. Lein Road becomes Burnside Road and has lots of mini bridges crossing the burn. Follow the single track road to the farm and then take the narrow path on the left.

What follows, as it gradually rises to about 100ft above the flood plain is – given reasonable weather – a panorama of the mouth of the Spey as it attempts to reach the sea. Just before you reach Garmouth there is a late 19th century water tower (above) and a little cluster of ancient standing stones; an indicator board explains all. You will emerge in Garmouth and return by the tar road. It is worth stopping to have a look across the burn at a reed bed. It is not exactly unique in Scotland, but very rare, especially on the East side of the country.

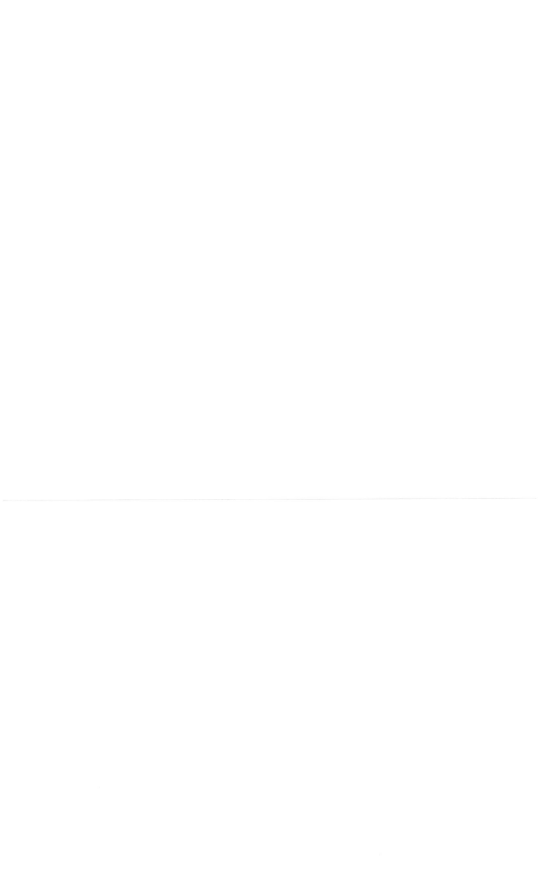

Appendix One

Golf on Speyside

Golf is an important component in the tourist industry of the Spey Valley, but it isn't only visitors who play the many courses in the area. Locals play as well and it's one of the oddities of the shinty-playing district that many of the best locals play cross-handed because that's the way they play shinty.

My expertise at golf is even more limited than my fishing skills, but I vividly remember the great Scottish golfers Eric Brown and John Panton playing a round at the Newtonmore club – it must have been in the 1950s – and being astounded when their drives reached the first green, all of 240 yards! We needed a good drive and a hefty three-iron to achieve the same thing. I guess these days Tiger Woods would use a pitching wedge.

Anyway, here are thumbnail sketches of many of the courses down the valley of the Spey. Prices are as of 2008.

Newtonmore: 6041yds, par 70. A good course for the modest golfer including a handy 'top four' (holes 1, 2, 17 and 18) for a late summer evening. £26.

Kingussie: 5643yds, par 67. Hilly, with spectacular layout beside the Gynack Burn below Creag Bheag (see also Walk 3). £26.

Aviemore has two courses. The **Delfaber Golf and Country Club**; nine-hole, 2436yds, par 32. Situated on parkland alongside the Spey. £10. And the **Spey Valley** course, opened in 2006. 7177yds, par 72. It has serious championship ambitions and claims the longest hole in Scotland, the 541yds 13th. £79.

Dufftown golf course

Carrbridge: Nine-hole, double round 5246yds, par 70. Course is forged out of the natural heath and moorland and even winds round a house that happened to be there. £16

Boat of Garten: 5876yds, par 70. Designed by the great James Baird and sometimes referred to as the 'Gleneagles of the North'. A serious course with wonderful views. £32.

Abernethy (Nethybridge): Nine-hole, double round 5068yds, par 66. Fairly kind if you ignore the pars. £18 per day.

Craggan (near Grantown): Recently cleverly upgraded from nine-hole to 18-hole. Short yardage makes it ideal for families, with snacks and meals and a trout fishery nearby (see Appendix Two). All holes are par three. Clubs for hire. Day fees are £20 for adults, £7 for children.

Grantown-on-Spey: 5710yds, par 70. A much-respected course. The ninth hole offers one of the best views in Strathspey. £28.

Ballindalloch Castle: Nine-hole but with different tees second time round. Double round 6495yds. Another beautiful setting, this time by the River Avon. £15/£20.

Dufftown: 5308yds, par 67. A fine challenge on sloping ground. If you have a right leg shorter than the left you will enjoy the outward half but struggle to stay upright on the way back. £15.

Rothes: Nine-hole, 2486yds, double round par 68. A parkland course fringed with forest. More fine views. £10.

Garmouth/Kingston: 6239yds, par 70. Mixture of parkland and links near the mouth of the Spey, looking out over the Moray Firth to distant Caithness. Parts used to be swept away by the river in spate, but no longer. £20

Spey Bay: 6230yds, par 70. Struggling (in 2008) because the associated hotel has closed. Facilities basic, but the course is in good condition. £20.

Other courses nearby include Keith, Buckpool, Strathlene and Cullen to the east and, on the other side, Moray New and Old at Lossiemouth, Elgin, Forres, Hopeman and Kinloss Nos 1 and 2.

Appendix Two
Fishing on a Budget

You may have gathered from the stories of seals (sort of) and eels, that I am not the world's greatest expert on the refined art of angling. And if you are the sort of person who is willing to pay hundreds, or even thousands, of pounds to fish the most exclusive beats of the River Spey, this is not the book for you.

But you do not have to be wealthy to fish the Spey and its tributaries and the lochs that are scattered thoughout Speyside. Here is a rough and ready guide to some of the fishing that is available at reasonable cost.

The Badenoch Angling Association manages and stocks a long section of the Spey from (and including) Spey Dam to the mouth of the Tromie below Kingussie, together with fishings on Lochs Laggan and Ericht. The association is based in Kingussie and permits are available from various outlets in Laggan, Newtonmore and Kingussie. Day tickets cost £10, season tickets are £35 for locals and £55 for visitors. Boat hire on Spey Dam (from Laggan Stores) costs £8 per session.

The Watersports Centre on Loch Insh offers tuition, tackle and fishing on the loch. Details from www.lochinsh.com.

Rothiemurchus Estate, near Aviemore, also offers tuition, tackle and fishing. One hour of fly-fishing instruction followed by an hour's fishing costs £35. A package of tuition, four hours of fishing and a complete set of rod, reel and line to take away costs £95.

The Strathspey Angling Improvement Association has the rights to long stretches of the Spey around Grantown. Permits cost £47 per day or £190 per week for visitors.

Craggan Fishery and Golf Course

Craggan Fishery and Golf Course, near Grantown has three fishing ponds, two bait ponds and a fly-fishing pond. Details from www.cragganforleisure.co.uk

With the Rivers Spey, Findhorn and Dulnain nearby, Carrbridge offers easy access to come excellent salmon fishing.

The Aberlour Angling Association has fishing on a mile-and-a-half stretch of the Spey from £20 per day or £100 per week. Details from their website.

Fochabers Angling Association also issue permits for the Spey costing between £20 and £65 per rod per day depending on the season. www.speyfishing fochabers.com

There are too many lochs in the area to mention here, but Bruce Sandison's *The Trout Lochs of Scotland* (Collins, 1987) has plenty of information and inspiration.

Appendix Three

The Story of Shinty

Shinty – or *Camanachd* as it is known in Gaelic – was introduced to Scotland from Ireland along with Christianity and the Gaelic language. And like the language, the game developed differently in the two countries, hurling in Ireland and shinty in Scotland. The two codes come together every year with representative matches played under composite rules.

There is some evidence that golf grew out of shinty players practising driving the ball long distances, and it is rather more certain that ice hockey in Canada was developed by shinty-playing Scottish immigrants.

Shinty may, at first glance, resemble hockey but the games are very different. Shinty is much faster, much more physical and has few restrictions on the use of the stick (caman), although deliberately hitting an opponent over the head is frowned upon. It is, as a result, rather more dangerous than hockey and more and more shinty players have taken to wearing helmets. It is compulsory for under-14 players to wear helmets.

Although a shinty pitch is roughly the same width as a football pitch at 70 to 80 yards, it is much longer, between 140 and 170 yards against 100 to 130 yards. So the players have to be fit as well as fierce.

Although shinty has some claim to be Scotland's national game – in the sense that it is unique to Scotland – its heartland is in the north and west of the country. We have already seen how sharp the dividing line is on Speyside between shinty and Highland League football (Chapter Seven).

Appendix Four

Speyside for Whisky

Why is Speyside home to almost 50 malt whisky distilleries, more than half of all the distilleries in Scotland?

Malt whisky can be made from only three ingredients – malted barley, yeast and pure water – and it is the ready availability of the barley and the water that makes Speyside the natural home of whisky distilling. The water doesn't come from the Spey itself but from the many burns and springs on the hillsides around the river.

The main crop traditionally grown by Scottish crofters was, of course, oats providing two of the staples of their diet – oatcakes (or bannocks) and porridge. But many crofters also had a small patch of barley which grew well in the fertile farmland of the Spey valley. Every farmer and crofter regarded it as his birthright to convert the crop into something to console him – and his family and friends – during the long, cold winters.

In the 17th century, the Scottish Parliament started taxing both malt and whisky and, following the Act of Union, taxation of whisky rose rapidly. Smuggling became widespread and – especially in the Highlands – socially acceptable. Ministers were known to hide the spirit under the pulpit and it was occasionally moved in coffins to avoid the excisemen, or guagers.

By the 1820s, despite the fact that up to 14,000 illicit stills were being

Strathisla Distillery

confiscated every year, more than half the whisky consumed in Scotland was enjoyed the more for having attracted no excise duty.

It was the Duke of Gordon who burst the smuggling bubble. He proposed that a regime should be introduced that allowed whisky to be produced profitably and legally. Following the Excise Act of 1823, many of the illicit stills turned legal and laid the foundations for the present Scotch whisky industry (see Chapter Six).

Although most whisky producers cannot guarantee that all their barley comes from Scotland, never mind from local farms, they use local grain as much as they can. Indeed some connoisseurs of whisky think the idea of using imported barley is as blasphemous as suggesting champagne needn't be made with French grapes. *Sacrebleu*!

Obviously the conditions for producing malt whisky are not confined to Speyside. There are distilleries the length and breadth of Scotland, from Islay in the south west to Shetland's newly established distillery in the far north. But Speyside remains the heartland of whisky. *Slainte Mha*!

Appendix Five
Flora and fauna of Speyside

I reckon I know a fair bit about the flora and fauna of the north of Scotland, but I also know my limitations. So I asked a proper expert on the subject, Dr Nigel Buxton, who has lived on Speyside for over 20 years for his summary of the plants and animals specific to the valley of the Spey. Here it is:

The valley of the Spey divides into three broad habitats: the river itself with its flood plain, marshes, grasslands and lochans; the woodlands; and the uplands, including some of Scotland's highest mountains with their sub-Arctic climate and vegetation.

The abundant vegetation in the first of these, including pondweeds and lilies, support many invertebrates like caddis flies and mayflies which is why the Spey and its tributaries are so important for salmon and trout and they, in turn, bring otters to the river and adjacent lochs.

The woodlands include both the remnants of the ancient wood of Caledon – for which Strathspey is best known – and broadleaf woods, mainly birch but with some oak, alder and bird cherry along the river itself. The presence of rare plants like the single-flowered wintergreen and the delicate twinflower testify to the undisturbed nature of these habitats, which are also home to rare mammals like the pine marten and red squirrel. The red squirrel is, as we know, severely threatened, but the pine marten is becoming, if not exactly common, at least well established in the area. More common mammals in the area include badgers, stoats and bats, especially pipistrelles, brown long-eared and Daubentons.

Spey Valley in Badenoch

The uplands have the heaths and blanket bog for which Scotland is world-renowned. This is the land of the heathers, the common heather or ling, the cross-leaved heather in wetter areas and the brightly coloured bell heather on drier areas and knolls. This is also red deer country and both here and in the woodlands there is the (slim) chance of seeing the secretive wild cat.

Arguably, however, it is for its birdlife that Speyside is best known. Badenoch is the centre of the breeding range of the goldeneye and the river is also home to the fish-eating goosander, the red-breasted merganser and an occasional widgeon. Dippers and grey wagtails are common as are lapwings, redshank and curlew with ringed plover and sandpipers appearing along the river edges. Merlin, osprey and hen harriers hunt the river and the fields and marshes alongside.

But it is in the pinewoods that the most distinctive birds are found. The crested tit and the Scottish crossbill are native to the area and the capercaillie, once common across Scotland following its re-introduction in the 19th century, is now largely restricted to Speyside and Deeside.

The uplands are, of course, home to peregrine falcons and golden eagles but they also support smaller, but no less interesting, species: golden plover, ptarmigan and dotterel with rare sightings of breeding snow buntings.

Around Spey Bay, the marine influence takes over with waders predominating – oystercatchers, dunlin and redshanks – and with seals, dolphins and whales out in the Moray Firth.

Places to visit include the following:

Spey Dam:	Goldeneye, grey-lag geese
Insh Marshes:	Breeding waders, goldeneye, whooper swan, hen harrier
Cairngorm National Nature Reserve:	Ptarmigan, dotterel, golden plover, golden eagle, snow bunting
Drakes Nursery, Inchriach:	Red squirrels
Rothiemurchus Fish Farm:	Osprey
Craigellachie National Nature Reserve:	Redstart, pied flycatcher
Abernethy Forest National Nature Reserve:	Crested tit, Scottish crossbill, capercaillie, osprey, grey-lag geese
Spey Bay:	Osprey, seaduck, great northern diver, red-throated diver, wintering waders, seals, cateceans

Appendix Six

Useful websites

This list is as complete as we can make it, but we would be glad to hear of any omissions. Information on locations not listed here can often be found on the Undiscovered Scotland website. (www.undiscoveredscotland.co.uk).

The quality of the sites various from brilliant to rudimentary. We leave you to work out which is which.

www.aviemore.co.uk
www.ballindallochcastle.co.uk
www.boatofgarten.com
www.carrbridge.com
www.clan-macpherson.org
www.clangrant.org
www.craigellachie.com
www.fochabers-heritage.org.uk
www.golfhighland.com
www.grantown.co.uk
www.grantownmuseum.co.uk
www.grantownonline.co.uk
www.heathercentre.com
www.kincraig.com
www.kingussie.com
www.knockandowoolmill.org.uk
www.laggan.com
www.landmark-centre.co.uk
www.lochinsh.com
www.moray.gov.uk/area/speyway
  (also includes pages for individual communities in Moray)
www.nethybridge.com
www.newtonmore.com
www.rspb.org
www.strathspeyrailway.co.uk
www.undiscoveredscotland.co.uk
www.visitaberlour.com
www.visitaviemore.com

Index

A

Aberlour 73–75
　Charles Grant 73
　Walkers 74–75
　fishing 114
Advie Church 68
Agricola 102
Alexander, James 93
Alvie Church 51
Alvie, Loch 51
Ardverikie Lodge 27
Aviemore 52–54
　Centre 53
　golf 111
Avon River 12–13, 69
　nearly meets the Don 12
　meets the Spey 13
Avon, Bridge of 69

B

Badenoch
　family connection 9
　Monarch of the Glen 32
　Kingussie only town 40
　James 'Ossian' Macpherson 44–45
　Angling Association 113
Balavil House 44
Balloch, The 102
Ballindalloch 69–70
　Avon meets Spey 13
　Castle 69
　golf 112
Balmoral 27
Balvenie Castle 21
Banchor, Glen
　family origins 9
　family evicted 31
　Cemetery 31
Banff 37–38
Beeching, Dr 52, 58
Bennachie 102
Ben Rinnes 73
Ben Nevis 20
Ben Vain 12
Boat of Garten 54–56
　golf 112
Boat O'Brig 90
British Alcan 10
Buchan Ness 102
Buckie
　Fishing Heritage Museum 104
　High School 93

Buckpool
　Start of Speyside Way 104
　golf 112
Burns, Robert 22

C

Cairngorms
　River Avon 12
　Moine Mhor 13
　Mountain Railway 53–54
　ski-ing 53
Cairn Gorm 12
Caithness 73
Calder, River
　swam in 9
　fishing 10, 27
　tributary of Spey 13
　Banchor Cemetery 31
Caledonian Pine Forest 52
Caledonii 102, 104
Calgacus 104
Caman 35, 85, 115
Cameron of Locheil 65
Cardhu 73, 76
Carrbridge 57–58
　Austrian Ski School 58
　World Porridge Championships 58
　golf 112
　fishing 114
Carron Bridge 80
Cathal's Stone 18
Cattanach, Calum 9
　two fine trout 10
　speaking Gaelic 10
Cattanach, Donald 31, 46
Cave of Raitts 43–44
Charlie, Bonnie Prince 19, 23
Christie, George 94
Claverhouse, John Graham of 65
Cluny Castle 27–28
　seat of Clan Macpherson 27
　Queen Victoria 27
Cluny's Cave 28–29
Cluny Macpherson 18, 28, 43
　daughter elopes 18
　'45 uprising 28
　died in France 28
Coire Ardair 17
Cooper, William Ltd 25
Cope, Gen Sir John 19–20
Corrieyairack Pass 18, 21
Craigellachie 73, 82

Speyside Way 80
Hotel 82
Speyside Cooperage 82
Craigellachie Bridge 81
Craggan Fishery & Golf 113
Creag Bheag 48
Creag Dubh
　Cluny's Cave 28
　Wild goats 28
　climbing 29
　hill race 35
　Macpherson war-cry 35
Creag Meaghaidh 17
Cromdale 66
　Battle of 66–67, 99
Crunachdan, Loch 20
Cullen 106
　golf 112
Cumming, Helen 76

D

Dalwhinnie 79
Delfur 87
Dodsworth, Ralph 24
Don, River 11, 68
　Avon nearly meets 12
Donald Ban 18
Drumochter 30, 79
Dufftown 85
　James MacPherson 38
　Whisky capital 85
　Whisky Festival 86
　golf 112
Dun na Lamh 21
Dunfermline House 101
Dunfermline Abbcy 101
Dulnain, River 57
　fishing 114
Dulnain 59
　Heather Centre 59
Dunbar, Lewis 55
Dundee 11
Dundee, Viscount 'Bonnie' 65
Dunkeld, Battle of 65

E

Eilean, Loch an 51
　osprey nest raid 55
Eilean Donan Castle 52
Elgin 75, 77
　Cathedral sacked 42
　golf 112

Ellan Bridge 57
Enzie, Brae of 102

F

Feshie, River 13, 51
  blocks Spey 15
Feshiebridge 9
Fiddich, River 82
Fiddichside Inn 82
Fife, Earl of 85
Fingal 44
Fingal's Cave 45
Findochty 25
Fochabers 90
  Baxters 91, 93
  by-pass 94
  canal 94
  Duke of Gordon 100, 118
  Museum 94
  fishing 114
Forres 42
  golf 112
Fort Augustus 18
Fort William 18, 20
Fraser, Sir Hugh 53

G

Galashiels 13
Garmouth 99
  King Charles II arrives 99
  Solemn League and
    Covenant 99
  port 100
  golf 112
Garry, River 65
Garten, Loch 54–55
  Osprey visitor centre 56
Garva 18
Garva Bridge 17, 19
Garvamore Barracks 19
Glenfarclas 73, 76
Glenfeshie 13, 46
Glenfiddich 75
Glenfinnan 19
Glen Grant 77, 86
Glenlivet 68
  whisky legalised 68
  distillery tour 75
Glen Moray 77
Glenmore 100
Gordon, Castle 87, 91, 94
Gordon, Duke and Duchess of
  establishes Kingussie 40
  monuments 51
  establishes Fochabers 90

Baxters 93
  sells timber 100
  legalising whisky 118
Gow, Neil 9
Grange, Pass of 102, 104
Grant, Anne 22
  Letters 22
  influence on Scott 23
  Edinburgh parade 23
Grant, Castle 64
Grant, Clan 64
  Clan gathering 58
Grant, 'Good' Sir James 63
Grantown-on-Spey 63
  history 63
  Queen Victoria 63
  Ramsay McDonald 63
  museum 64
  golf 112
  fishing 113
Gurkha Bridge 57
Gynack, River 41

H

Highland Folk Museum
  kit school and church 25
  Newtonmore site 36
  Cattanach plaid 46
Highland Wildlife Park 45
Highlander Inn 82
Hogg, James 'Ettrick Shepherd' 67

I

Insh Church 46
Insh Marshes 15, 41, 121
Insh, Loch Watersports 49
  fishing 113
Inveravon Church 73
  Pictish stones 74
Invernahavon, Battle of 29–30
Inverness 11
  night train to London 9
Inverurie 13

J

Jacobites 64–67
  Risings 18, 41
  Hey, Johnnie Cope 20
  Clan Grant 64
Jones, Hugh 79

K

Kelso 13
Killiecrankie, Battle of 65, 86
King Charles II 16

Intrigue following death 64
King George IV fan of Scott 23
  parade in Edinburgh 23
  tartan 23
  samples whisky 68
King James II/VII 64
Kincraig 45
Kingston 100–101
  at mouth of Spey 101
  shipbuilding 100–101
Kingussie 35, 39–41
  dances 9
  shinty 35
  Duke of Gordon 40
  history 40
  railway arrives 40
  Ruthven Barracks 41
  The Dell 41
  Victorians 40
  golf 111
  fishing 13
Knockando Wool Mill 79

L

Laggan 21–23, 27
  Anne Grant 22
  church 22
  kit house near 25
  doctors 27
  fishing 113
Laggan Bridge 22
Laggan, Loch picnics 9
  Spey diverted via 20
  Ardverikie lodge 27
Laichie 85
Lanark 13
Landmark Adventure Centre 58
Lecht 100
Lethendry Castle 66
Linnhe, Loch 21
Lochy, Loch 21

M

Mashie, River 22
Macallan, The 73, 82
McBride, Marylou 74
McKay, Dr Kenneth 27
MacKenzie, Donald 98
Macpherson, Clan Cluny Castle 27
  Chief called Cluny 28
  Cattanachs and 31
  Gathering 35
  Museum 32, 36–38
MacPherson, James 36–39
  fiddle in museum 37

THE SPEY: FROM SOURCE TO SEA

captured 37
hanged 38
song MacPherson's Rant 39
Macpherson, James 'Ossian' 44
Goethe 44
Mendelssohn 45
Napoleon 45
Dr Samuel Johnson 45
Marshall, William 93
Meall na Cuaich 30–31
Melrose 13
Mendelssohn 45
Millar, Peter 88
Milne, Alexander 91
Moine Mhor 13
Monadhliath Mountains
source of Spey 15
Cromdale viewpoint 66
Mons Graupius, Battle of 102–104
Moray Firth 12, 15
Moray Coastal Trail 104–106
fishing 101
Wildlife Centre 108
wildlife 120
Morlich, Loch picnics 9
Mosstodloch Baxters 91
Muckle Spate 57, 68, 82

N

Nether Dallachy 102
Nethybridge 58
Clan Grant Gathering 58
Highland Games 58
Abernethy Forest 59
golf 112
New Zealand kit houses 25
Abernethy Games and 58
Newtonmore 9–10
family moved to 9
moving train 9
Clan Macpherson gathering 35
Clan Macpherson Museum 36
Eilan 35
village established 31
Highland Games 35
Highland Folk Museum 36
rivalry with Kingussie 35
shinty 35
golf 111

O

Ordiquish 90
Orton earth pillars 90
experiment 11
estate 87–90
Osborne, William 100

P

Packhorse Bridge 57, 68, 83
Carrbridge 57
Glenlivet 68
Perth 11
Battle of Mons Graupius 102
Picts Dun na Lamh 21
stones 68, 73
Pitmain Inn 39
Pluscaden Abbey destroyed by Wolf 42
Portessie 104
Portknockie 106
Portsoy 106
Ptarmigan 120

R

Revak Estate 64
Red Corff House 101
Rhìne, River 11
Richardson, Dr Iain 27
Richmond and Gordon, Duke 94
Rinnes, Ben 73
Rothes 86–87
Castle 86
golf 112
Rothiemurchus Scots Pine habitat 61
fishing 113
Ruthven Barracks Comyn Earls 41
Jacobites 41
Wolf of Badenoch 42

S

Sandend 106
Shinty 115
rivalry 35
Eilan 35
The Dell 41
Skinner, Scott 93
Sluggan Bridge 57
Spey Bay 98
ecology 104
nature reserve 108
golf 112
Spey Dam 20–21
fishing 113
Spey Floaters 101
Spey, Loch source of Spey 17–18
trout 15
Spey Viaduct 98
Speybank 51
Speyfest 94
Speyside Heather Centre 59
Speyside High School 74
Speyside Way Boat of Garten 56
Cromdale 67
Aberlour 75
Ballindalloch to Craigellachie 80

Dufftown 85
Fochabers to Spey Bay 98
final stretch 104
Speirs, R.R & Co 25
Staffa 45
Stirling 13
Strath Avon 68
Strathisla 77
Strathmashie 21
Strathspey Railway 53–54

T

Tacitus 102–104
Telford, Thomas Sluggan Bridge 57
Craigellachie Bridge 81–82
Tomintoul Speyside Way 73
manganese 100
Tormore Distillery 69
Treig, Loch 20
Tromie, River tributary 13
fishing 113
Truim tributary 13
Dalwhinnie distillery 79
fishing the falls 97
Tugnet 11, 106

U

Urquhart Priory 101

V

Victoria, Queen Highland hideaways 27
visits Grantown 63
Victoria Bridge 80

W

Wade, General George 18–19
Ruthven Barracks 41
Carrbridge 57
Walkers of Aberlour 74–75
Wester Elchies 80
William the Lyon 18
Wolf of Badenoch 42–43
Loch an Eilean 51–52

Luath Press Limited

committed to publishing well written books worth reading

LUATH PRESS takes its name from Robert Burns, whose little collie Luath (*Gael.*, swift or nimble) tripped up Jean Armour at a wedding and gave him the chance to speak to the woman who was to be his wife and the abiding love of his life. Burns called one of 'The Twa Dogs' Luath after Cuchullin's hunting dog in Ossian's *Fingal*. Luath Press was established in 1981 in the heart of Burns country, and is now based a few steps up the road from Burns' first lodgings on Edinburgh's Royal Mile.

Luath offers you distinctive writing with a hint of unexpected pleasures.

Most bookshops in the UK, the US, Canada, Australia, New Zealand and parts of Europe either carry our books in stock or can order them for you. To order direct from us, please send a £sterling cheque, postal order, international money order or your credit card details (number, address of cardholder and expiry date) to us at the address below. Please add post and packing as follows: UK – £1.00 per delivery address; overseas surface mail – £2.50 per delivery address; overseas airmail – £3.50 for the first book to each delivery address, plus £1.00 for each additional book by airmail to the same address. If your order is a gift, we will happily enclose your card or message at no extra charge.

Luath Press Limited
543/2 Castlehill
The Royal Mile
Edinburgh EH1 2ND
Scotland
Telephone: 0131 225 4326 (24 hours)
Fax: 0131 225 4324
email: sales@luath.co.uk
Website: www.luath.co.uk